New World Extra

Books by Joe David Bellamy

Fiction
Suzi Sinzinnati
Atomic Love

Nonfiction
Literary Luxuries
The New Fiction
American Poetry Observed
The Bellamys of Early Virginia
The Lost Saranac Interviews

Poetry
Olympic Gold Medalist
The Frozen Sea

Anthologies
Apocalpyse
SuperFiction
Moral Fiction
New Writers for the Eighties
Love Stories/Love Poems

New World Extra

Joe David Bellamy

Bellamy
House

New World Extra

Copyright © 2009 by Joe David Bellamy

All rights reserved. No part of this book may be used or reproduced by any means, graphic, electronic, or mechanical, including photocopying, recording, taping, or by any information storage retrieval system without the written permission of the publisher except in the case of brief quotations embodied in critical articles or reviews.

Bellamy House Publishing
5318 Lake Bluff Terrace
Sanford, FL 32771

www.joedavidbellamy.com

First Edition

Cover photo © Joe David Bellamy from view of pond at First Landing State Park, Virginia Beach, Virginia, near the site where the Jamestown party came ashore at Cape Henry in 1607.

ISBN 978-0-578-02509-4

Printed in the United States of America

Connie Sue

"*The New World* is a sweeping adventure set amidst the first encounter of European and American cultures during the founding of the Jamestown Virginia settlement in 1607. Acclaimed filmmaker Terrence Malick brings to life his own unique interpretation of the classic tale of Pocahontas and her relationships with adventurer John Smith and aristocrat John Rolfe. This woman's remarkable journey of love lost and found takes her from the untouched beauty of the Virginia wilderness to the upper crust of English society as we witness the dawn of a new America.

In the early years of the 17th century, North America is much as it has been for the previous five thousand years—a vast land of seemingly endless primeval wilderness populated by an intricate network of tribal cultures. Although these nations live in graceful harmony with their environment, their relations with each other are a bit more uneasy. All it will take to upset the balance is an intrusion from the outside.
One is not long in coming."

◼ New Line Cinema synopsis

Dramatis Personae

Terrence Malick……………….……………..Writer/Director

Jacqueline West……………………………Costume Designer

Colin Farrell……………...………..……..Capt. John Smith

Christopher Plummer………….……Capt. Christopher Newport

Qorianka Kilcher……………..…………..……….Pocahontas

Yorick Van Wageningen……….……..……………….Argall

Christian Bale……………………………………John Rolfe

David Thewlis…………………………………….Wingfield

Ben Mendelsohn……………………………….…..…Ben

Joe David Bellamy……………..………………......an extra

1

Virginia Beach, Virginia: I see in the newspaper they are filming a movie up on the Peninsula, and it's going to be called *The New World*. It's a different take on the story of the Jamestown Colony—with Colin Farrell as Capt. John Smith and Christopher Plummer as Capt. Christopher Newport. The paper says it is the biggest production ever to be filmed in Virginia!

They are putting out a casting call for extras! I drive up on a rainy day and wait with a long line of people in what looks like a junior high gymnasium. I decide, after checking out the crowd of applicants, most of whom are young women with elaborate hairdos, that I am probably too old for this job. (In real life, I am a professor and a writer, but I decide to keep that to myself.) I fill out a form with my height and weight and give them my picture with a little note attached mentioning that my ancestor Edward Spalding was actually a resident of Jamestown, which is probably my only qualification for this job. I have never been in a film before.

When I go up to the table, the casting director says she "loves my look." What look is that, I wonder—completely unpremeditated? Then I turn the wrong way going out of the parking lot and drive around for an hour or so, lost back in the deep woods of Charles City County, Virginia, which must look today pretty much as it did when so many of the colonists in Jamestown, just to the south, died there.

Several weeks pass with no word at all. Then one day, the Virginia casting director for *The New World* calls and invites me to be a stand-in the next day for Christopher Plummer. She says I am exactly the same height and weight as he is—lucky me. I will receive $10/hour and be considered a member of the crew, which means I will be permitted to eat with the crew. I'm not exactly sure what a stand-in is or why I would want to eat with the crew, but I agree to do it and she gives me an elaborate schedule for when I will need to be on the set over the next several weeks.

Later that same day the casting director calls back and says they won't need me tomorrow after all. They are shooting on the ship, and the space is too small for stand-ins. She is sorry but she often doesn't get the next day's shooting schedule until that late. She is sure they will use me again. If I want to, she says, I can drive up in the morning anyway and look around and meet some people. I say, "Okay."

Once I leave the Interstate, the roads on my map take me farther and farther from civilization. Small towns give way to corn fields, horse farms, and then dense wooded sections. At each turn, as the roads become smaller and harder-to-find, someone has posted a small, helpful sign with bright red letters "TNW." Little do most of the other travelers know that these letters signify *The*

New World, a major film happening right here, right now.

From the description the casting director has given me, I expect to be able to park in a parking lot. But the base camp for the production is actually out in the middle of an immense, deep, almost primeval, forest, and cars, pick-ups, and SUVs are parked along the pot-holed road leading up to the base camp for a mile or so. So I park and hike the last mile.

What I find when I arrive is a teaming mass of semis and aluminum trailer-buildings and tents parked and erected practically on top of one another in a semi-circle in a gravel clearing hewed out of the woods. Heavy electrical cables are snaking everywhere underfoot, so that the whole place hums. Some people are getting food from a vendor-type truck and a few people are milling around. Everyone seems to know what they are doing except me. I ask someone where casting is, and they point me politely to the right place.

Casting is a kind of metal building made out of double-wides. It has real windows and air conditioners and a central hall with several large rooms to either side. One of them is labeled to indicate it is a dining room for the crew, and another is a dining room for the extras. These are empty at present. There are some people gathered in another room that says "Extras Casting," so I go in there.

Eventually I find Jeannie, the casting director. Jeannie apologizes again for the false alarm, and I say not to worry. I am adaptable. I remind her that one of my ancestors was actually a resident of Jamestown in 1619 and had survived the Indian massacre of 1622. I imply that I am made out of similar stuff. I am curious, I say, to see what it feels like to be out here in the woods the way my ancestor had been, which was the reason I had accepted.

Jeannie takes me on a mini-tour of the camp and introduces me here and there as we pass. I meet Jackie West from wardrobe, who is an unassuming woman with her hair pulled back. I meet an assistant director, who is an Indian woman, and a black woman named Shirelle, who is a PA, whatever that is. Jeannie introduces me to everyone as "the new stand-in for Christopher Plummer."

As I am preparing to leave, she tells me, confidentially, that the first stand-in for Christopher Plummer had been fired after only one day because he was too talkative. He seemed perfect because "he looked just like Plummer," but he tried to schmooze with Plummer and with the director and had even offered advice to the director, which, she implies, is a serious breach of movie-making etiquette. Stand-ins just don't do that. "He was just too chummy," she says. I should be advised that Plummer is something of a curmudgeon and that—in so many words—the best course of action is to do what I am told and to keep my mouth shut. I say I understand perfectly and that she can count on my discretion.

Days pass. There follows a series of calls from Jeannie in which she says—each call—that the schedule is being revised and my services as a stand-in are not needed that day after all. Then one day she calls and says they still don't need me as a stand-in, but how would I like to work as an extra the next day? That way I could actually be on camera and be *in* the movie. I say sure. Who would pass up that kind of opportunity for immortality?

My wardrobe fitting is a separate trip, but, luckily, I don't have to be there until 1:30 in the afternoon. It's a long drive. The base camp is mostly deserted, as the majority of the actors and crew are still out on the set. The wind is blowing and scattered showers are predicted. I proceed to the wardrobe tent, where I am at the mercy of Jackie West, whom I had met previously, and Suzie. Jackie gives me some hangers with a blousy shirt and a pair of wool cut-off trousers and a sack with new shoes and long knee socks in it—also a leather belt with a pouch. Jackie says to put it all on and they'll be back.

I can see myself turning into a 17th century man in the mirrors around the sides of the tent, but the shirt doesn't fit. As the wind blows outside and rain pelts against the tent, the canvas flaps and the mirrors, which are fastened to it, bounce and roll, making everything seem a little surreal. Jackie comes back in with a suede coat. I try it on, and it's too small too—not even close. She takes my measurements again, as if she can't believe I am as big as I seem to be, and goes back out. Her next coat is also too small—I can't get my hands through the sleeves. Jackie helps me by pulling at it, but it's really hopeless. "I lift weights," I say. "Maybe my proportions are different." Suzie whispers something into Jackie's ear. They both go out.

When they come back, they have a new shirt and a vest. The shirt isn't quite as bright or ornate, but the fit is better, and the vest goes on quite nicely. It's dark brown wool but looks like leather. The women seem relieved. There is also a dark reddish brown velvet hat with a feather in it. We try it on at various angles—it's hard to tell which is front or back.

Suzie kneels down and works at tying my leggings together with the little rawhide strings attached. Then she stands up and unloosens the end of my belt and loops it a different way around by my side-pouch. The women fluff me and tie the string at my neck that holds my shirt together in the front. "Those shoes are too new-looking," Suzie says. "You should rub dirt on them or walk through some puddles as soon as you get to the set." Then Jackie takes out a camera and snaps my picture.

It is only later on that I realize who Jackie West is. I had taken her to be a very sweet, modest woman who couldn't get my measurements right. Later, I find out she designed the costumes for the whole movie and probably made them from scratch as well (with the help of her staff), right down to my shoes. Jackie West is an Oscar nominee and is world-renowned for costume design! Her name is way up in the credits, right next to Malick's, because she is an extremely talented and important woman. The only reason they had some trouble fitting me was probably because they had only a few items of apparel left lying around without making up an entirely new costume. Everyone else had been fitted already, and I was just an extra who came late.

I find out soon enough why it is desirable to be able to eat with the crew. The crew actually has a catered menu of real food. For example, the crew gets to have breakfasts-to-order at the vendor food-truck in the morning while the extras get runny oatmeal and Pop-tarts back in the casting building. At lunch, the crew gets to eat first while the extras have to wait and then eat what's left very quickly. It's definitely better to be considered a member of the crew. But I am not. If I had been a stand-in, I would have been. But as an extra, I am just one of the rabble. Jeannie seems to have forgotten to mention this to me.
It is not until I receive my first check in the mail that I realize I am not receiving $10 an hour either, as I had been promised originally, but just over half that--$5.35/hour. No one has thought it a priority to mention this to me either. Of course, I am not doing what I was invited to do either but a thing that is far more difficult and rewarding—trying to *act*, trying to actually *be in the picture*. So what am I complaining about?

2

My first day as an extra: it is an afternoon call. I check in with Jane in casting and then go to the wardrobe tent and give them my paperwork and am presented with my colonist's outfit and bag. I get dressed with some of the other extras who are in the same scene and then proceed to hair and make-up, which is in the same big tent.

First is hair. The hair woman says, "Get ready to lose ten years," and then sprays dark-colored dye on my hair and sideburns. She is right—I look younger already, but will this stuff ever come out, I wonder? When she is finished I move over to the other side of the long table and sit down on a stool, and the make-up woman goes to work on my face. "You aren't going to be quite as dirty as the others," she says, "You're to be something of a gentleman."

"Okay," I say, as if I have a choice. Still she is spraying me with a black-looking mist that smells like alcohol. She puts it on my face and hands, on my arms up to the elbows, and on my chest and neck. It's cold. Then she works on my eyes and cheeks with sponges and a brush. When she is finished, I look colorful but dangerous. If this is less dirty-looking, I think as I look at myself in the mirror, the others must be filthy!

Shirelle, the PA (production assistant) assigned to us, is in a hurry to move us to the prop van. She hustles us into a waiting golf cart, accelerates, and sends us caroming down the humped dirt road out toward the wilderness. Everyone's hair is flying in the wind. She pulls up in a leafy spot beneath some big trees where a semi trailer is parked. "Get them propped up so we can move," she says to the guy waiting there. "We're running late."

"Sure thing," he says. Shirelle goes zooming off in her hotrod golf cart.

I realize the semi trailer is full of swords and muskets and armor and knives and all kinds of assorted weaponry—pikes, clubs, crossbows, you name it. The prop guy is a real hard-ass who outfits us as he sees fit. One gets a small crossbow, one a dagger. I receive a sword and a dagger, each in its own holster for suspending from my belt. The sword is big. I have to take my belt off and adjust my leather bag to the other side to accommodate the sword, since it has to swing from my left hip (according to the prop guy) so that I can reach across with my right hand to yank it out in case of emergency. Once I am strapped up properly, I begin to feel a new sense of authenticity and panache. Now I am clearly someone to reckon with. Who would dare to cross a man so well-endowed with steel? With a sword this big, you generally don't have to use it. You just walk into a room, and everyone is unusually polite and deferential. I like the feeling already.

The prop guy is in the middle of a tyrannical lecture about how we should never, never, under any circumstances, remove our weapons from their holsters or scabbards—because if we do, someone will be injured! He guarantees it!

Suddenly Shirelle is back at our sides, urging us to hop aboard her careening golf cart. The prop guy yells at our backs to return all props to the truck at day's end or face certain death. Back at the base camp, the other colonists and several Indians and crew have just finished lunch. Shirelle loads the extras into the back of a stake-bed truck, and we stand together like a bunch of prisoners on our way to Sing-Sing. (The crew gets to use a cushy van.) The truck chugs off back down the humped dirt road, but this time we are going to the set, bouncing and dodging low-hanging branches as we ride. I have nothing to fear from the several Indians crammed in amongst us because I am well-armed and may be dangerous myself.

The truck pulls up to a row of porta-potties and we climb down. We head up a path past some tables where other extras are hanging about and munching nut bars and drinking bottled water. The path opens out into a wide field adjacent to the Chickahominy River. Gnarled trees line the riverbank to our right. Ahead we see what looks like an encampment, first a small circus-like tent, then a wall of logs, like the half-built side of a fort. In the distance are lean-tos and small log buildings and more tents, and a wide field beyond is filled with tassels of vegetation. The whole is encircled by deep forest.

We loiter for a while, getting our bearings, as members of the crew begin to appear. There is no place to sit, unless you want to risk chiggers. Suddenly everyone is there, including Colin Farrell and Christopher Plummer, and we are ready to begin. Our director, Terrence Malick, is the large man in the straw hat who has been conferring for some time with a man named Joerg, who, it turns out, is the cameraman. Joerg is slender but athletic, which is a good thing, because he has to carry an enormous camera strapped between his shoulder blades.

Plummer is a man who exudes presence and gravitas, and I can understand why when I learn later on that he is the grandson and great grandson of two Canadian prime ministers. He is 75 years old but still seems muscular and agile for his years. He is well-cast to be a leader.

Colin Farrell has shoulder-length black hair and a full beard for this film, which gives him an entirely different look from his appearance in *Phone Booth.* In person, he seems quite a bit more handsome than I expected, and there is an aura about him that is not just due to the fact that everyone knows he is famous. He is magnetic—someone you have to look at—though my fellow extras and I are trying to be cool about it. Someone discovered him in a play in Dublin when he was in his early twenties, and now he's a star. I guess that kind of talent is rare enough that if you've got it, someone finds out.

Another very striking fellow is the actor Yorick Van Wageningen, who plays Argall and is Dutch. He has the distinctive and rugged look of a medieval hero, but he could be a linebacker for the Green Bay Packers. He is wearing a yoke of armor that encircles his neck, and it enhances his already powerful physical presence. So we have a Canadian, an Irishman, and a Dutchman to play the leading men at the English colony of Jamestown. Is this a coincidence or are American actors just too casual and modern—lacking the necessary classical preparation to play this historical period piece? Don't ask me.

New World Extra

3

Yorick Van Wageningen

The director says he wants us to walk together up this slight incline into the heart of the camp, and Christopher Plummer will be giving us a little tour, talking as we go, bringing us up-to-date on changes and developments in the colony. The five extras in our group have apparently just arrived from England, but we are men of some distinction referred to in the script as the "Jamestown elders." Plummer will be turning to face us periodically as he leads the procession.

Yorick will walk at the front, and Colin will walk on my right. Joerg will be back-peddling up the slope, filming us over Plummer's head with his mongo shoulder-mounted camera and trying not to fall down. "Let's rehearse it a few times," Malick says.

We converge and start trooping up the path toward camp while Plummer supplies the monologue and an agile Asian man with a boom on a long pole struggles to keep pace. The extras are jockeying for the best angle in order to plant a piece of their fleeting mugs in the middle of the camera's eye. I have gotten myself just behind Yorick, and he is so large that I can't see the camera at all at first; and if I can't see the camera, the camera can't see me.

The trouble is that when I try to move to Yorick's left side for a better vantage point, I am in serious danger of impaling my loins on Yorick's sword, which is tilted backwards and bobs up and down as he walks over the uneven ground. There are several starts and stops and others pressing in behind me, and, of course, I am also pretending to listen to everything Plummer is saying to us. But I have to be especially careful to stop when Yorick does or I am done for. There is no alternative to risking my life at the end of Yorick's sword if I want to be on camera, so, of course, I do.

When we reach the top of the incline—in sight of the camp flag—our director decides he wants us to do an abrupt about face and walk back down the same way we have come. Now Joerg is filming us from behind, but he doesn't want to be too far behind, so as Plummer splits the tide and walks back down and the column rotates and Yorick's sword bounces dangerously in front of me, I find I am running into the side of the camera as Joerg closes in quickly from behind us.

Joerg can't really see me because his eye is glued to the

image he is filming, and I can't seem to turn fast enough to stay in front of him because so many bodies are pressing against me from behind. Gradually we work this out as we keep rehearsing, and mainly it is done simply by forcing one's way into position at exactly the right moment and letting the other bodies know you will be occupying a particular space and they will have to adjust accordingly. What surprises me is that the extras have so much latitude to decide where they will go and what they will do. We each create within our own little microcosm of opportunity.

Finally, after about five tries, the director decides we are ready to convert rehearsal to the real thing. Now we will be burning real celluloid, even if most of it will end up on the cutting room floor. Time for a short break to collect our wits. Everyone but Plummer and I taps out a cig and gets a quick nicotine hit, even the guy in full armor. Cups and bottles of water are passed around. One of the make-up men walks up to me and without saying anything starts dabbing at my eyes with a sponge. Does he want the bags under my eyes to show up more starkly or to recede? I wait patiently.

Then we hear the call "Clear the set," and there is a mad scramble to dispose of the butts and plastic cups. Helpful crew members hold out pails and boxes to collect the debris—we wouldn't want to ruin the credibility of the scene because of the flagrant appearance of a half-full 21st century bottle of Poland Spring in the middle of a 17th century briefing by Captain Christopher Newport.

We line up and someone calls out, "Clear the set! Rolling, rolling, rolling—action!" Here we go. This is it. We do the scene again about ten times, stopping occasionally for planes overhead, for film at the end of its roll, for motorboats on the river that have eluded blockades, and for more cigs. By now I have most of Plummer's long, long speech memorized. My muscles are locked in to all the movements necessary. I am best at about take four or five. After that, I am trying harder and harder to act as if this is all spontaneous. I find I am concentrating most of my acting power, such as it is, on trying to avoid projecting boredom. I'm not sure I am succeeding.

Then the director wants to try a new wrinkle. He adds another camera. As we walk back down the slope, this second camera is grinding away on our right side, and I make the assumption that they are honing in on Colin Farrell who is walking beside me now within arm's reach on my left and who is, after all, the star. So I fall back a pace or two in order to give this right hand camera a favorable angle on Colin's profile. At the last moment, an invisible hand grabs me from behind and pushes me forward. Instinctively, I rubberneck around to see who is molesting me. The blond female drill sergeant who is running things yells, "Cut!"

Apparently, I have messed up big time and ruined the scene. If you are grabbed by an invisible hand, you are not supposed to react—this is a rule that everyone is supposed to know. She lets me have it with both barrels. What do they expect when they take strangers off the street, pay them $5.35/hour, and line them up next to Colin Farrell and Christopher Plummer and expect them to act! This happens two or three more times—when we reach the spot at the bottom of the hill, a hand reaches out and pushes me forward and I go where it places me without turning around.

At the next break, I mumble something about "Who was that woman who grabbed me from behind?" to no one in particular, and Yorick says: "But the real question is: Did you *like* it?" and laughs heartily. Finally the pushing person gets the bright idea of asking me why I am doing what I am doing. Then I tell her I'm trying to get out of the way of the shot on Colin, and she tells me they are also shooting from behind and by moving out of the way I am leaving a hole in the tableau. I need to move up. Oh, okay. Now I get it. It's amazing what a little verbal communication can accomplish. We do several more takes with me walking precisely where I am supposed to walk and stopping in precisely the right spot.

The light is shifting. The day is drawing to a close. We have been working for *hours*. We take another break, and

Christopher Plummer whips out his cell phone, and I hear him place a call to the Williamsburg Inn to check on his accommodations. The water bottles and cigs come out again all around, and one of the wardrobe girls is patting my shoes with a veneer of dust—they are still too new-looking. Through all of these struggles, we are bonding with one another.

Plummer seems to me not to be "a curmudgeon" at all but rather a consummate professional who reminds me of my father. He is able to say his lines over and over again without faltering and make it seem as if it is the first time *every* time. After a day of working together, we have become something like colleagues and he gives me an occasional approving smile. I am, after all, one of the few adults on the set who is anywhere near his age (not to mention exactly his height and weight), and I am just trying to do my job, the same as he is. The snack crew is passing out goodies, but the best nut bars are all gone before the basket reaches me. Oh well. I try to eat a few salty-tasting sunflower seeds but spit them out because the hulls are still on.

Now it is dusk and Colin and I are standing next to the Chickahominy and gazing out across the darkening water toward the ship. The shadows of gnarled trees grow long around us. Possibly we are thinking about home and the people we have left behind in this lavender light. The air around Colin Farrell is bright with regret and longing—though he does not say a word. The camera behind us is grinding away, and I may not be in the picture at all—or just a blob to the side. But I try to live in the moment, just in case this is the scene that will survive.

I glance at the sword and dagger on my belt. Both are a little rusty but still impressive. My dagger is about a foot and a half long, and the sword has an intricate handle of curving interlaced strips to protect my hand from slashing if I should find myself in a sword fight. I am altogether pleased with them until I see the sword and dagger set that Colin Farrell has on.

His are bright polished steel with pearl handles, and there is not a spot of rust on them. I confess to a moment of sword and dagger envy there in the twilight. This is perhaps one obvious difference between the actor who makes $20 million and has his own trailer and the actor who makes $5.35/hour and who has to wait in line after the crew is finished before he is permitted to eat a bite of lunch. One of us gets to carry niftier props!

4

Finally one of the blond drill sergeants makes an announcement in the distance up by the tent, and those of us who are too far away to hear assume it is the signal that we are dismissed. Several of the extras amble up that way, and I can see them tossing their weapons into the tent. I distinctly remember that the prop guy told us to bring his props back to the truck or die. I ask one of the guys, Randy, on the way out, and Randy says he doesn't know. All he knows is that he has to be back first thing in the morning, and everyone else was tossing their stuff, and he is dog-tired.

Well, *okay*, I think, *I wasn't invited back first thing in the morning, but at least I can follow instructions.* No way I am going to give up my sword and dagger just because everyone else is doing it. As we are filing out on the dark path, Jane from casting grabs my arm and says, "Are you sure it's okay to leave?" She is in the middle of eating a nut bar. Jane is about 6' 2" with naturally curly blond hair down to her shoulders.

"I think so," I say.

"How do you know?"

"The blond woman said something," I say.

"Who was she? Was she an Assistant Director?"

"I don't know who she was."

"You'd better stay. I don't think you're supposed to leave yet."

"But everyone is leaving," I say. Up ahead I can see Randy and the other extras are already on board the stake-bed and the taillights and yellow cab lights are glowing. They are about to pull away.

"Hang on right here," Jane says, cramming in the last of her candy, "and I'll go back and find out what's going on." She does a pick-and-roll and disappears into the darkness. *This is absurd*, I am thinking as the stake-bed pulls away, leaving a stench of exhaust fumes in its wake. *How am I going to get back?* I feel like the kid who missed the school bus.

While I am waiting for Jane, one of the Indians approaches and looks me up and down. He is about eighteen with shoulder-length hair, and he has a beaded headband and a droll, unreadable expression on his face. He asks me if he can check out my sword. I say, "Sure," not realizing he means to take it out of the scabbard. Before I can stop him, he jerks the sword out and swishes and flashes it around in the waning light. Then he brandishes it at me, as if I had been his quarry all along. His expression goes from mildly respectful to wild and maniacal. I think he is probably putting me on, but I have the distinct impression that he may be about to run me through with my own sword. What a way to die! How do I know he isn't crazy? How do I know if he is even a real Indian? After a little more fooling around, he hands it back to me.

"Thanks," he says. He gives me a little salute and disappears down the path.

I wait for ten minutes by the side of the porta-potties, and when Jane returns she has the startling news that sure enough, "It's okay to leave."

"The truck already left," I say. "Should I walk back?"

"You can ride in my golf cart," she says.

On the way back, Jane tells me her life story. This is one effect I often have on people—I don't know why except that I am perhaps too attentive, a trait that served me well in grade school. Jane is almost thirty. She is the mother of three, and she lives in Richmond. She is 6' 2" and played some basketball, she admits, but claims she wasn't any good. (*Just modest*, I think, *still mad at herself for missing some foul shot a decade ago*.) Now she is a part-time actress.

She's been on HBO a few times, in small roles. Mostly she does commercials these days, and sometimes she goes as far as Baltimore to do them. I express complete amazement that someone living in Richmond is able to have a professional life as an actress, but she says it's possible, it's entirely possible. *It probably doesn't hurt to be big and beautiful and to have lovely hair*, I think (but, of course, do not say).

"Have you seen Pocahontas yet?" I ask. "I hear they had a hard time finding her."

"Yes, she's lovely, a very pretty girl—quite tiny though."

"I imagine most people seem tiny to you."

"No, she really is tiny."

"Can she act though?"

"I hear they're very pleased with her. I hear she's acting her butt off!"

"That's good!"

Back at the casting building, it is mostly deserted by now but bright as an airline terminal. Shirelle is pacing the floor, waiting for the extras to file in. She says I have to wait until the others return so that we can all carry our props back to the prop van. I doubt seriously that the prop guy is still out there in the middle of the pitch black darkness at this hour.

I tell her I am the only one left, and I am the only one who brought my weapons back. Shirelle comes unhinged by this news. She says we were instructed in no uncertain terms to bring our props back to the van and that is what she expects, and I say that is exactly why I brought mine back—so that they could be delivered to the van, as specified. But, unfortunately, the other guys didn't. I had no control over that. They pitched them into the tent out on the set, and now they are gone. Jane, who senses a confrontation, slips quickly away.

"Well, that's too bad," Shirelle says. "You're just going to have to wait until they all get here."

"They aren't coming back!" I say. "They're gone! I'm the only one who did what I was told. I'm going home!" I unleash my belt and throw the sword and dagger onto the table, where they land with a huge bang and a clatter, and I stomp out and keep on walking. I am amazed at my own anger, but I am really losing patience with this movie-making madness! I haven't eaten in eight hours, and it's pushing ten o'clock at night. I still have a long drive ahead of me, and I have to hike a mile to my car in a pitch-dark, bug-infested wilderness! This may be the end of my film career, but I can't help it. Sometimes you just flip out!

5

Today, I have to get out of bed at 4:30 A.M. You wouldn't believe how much traffic there is on the Interstate at five in the morning. I drive to the movie in a kind of dream, grateful for each of the small TNW signs, and am pleased to see, when I arrive, that I am amongst the earliest arrivals so I can park my car just a short walk from the base camp.

But when I turn the corner, expecting the usual set-up, the place is almost entirely deserted! It's just an acre of gravel and the casting building and the vendor truck, and the hum is missing because most of the trailers are gone. "Where is everything?" I say in astonishment to my old friend Jane who is sitting out front.

"They moved to the Indian camp today," Jane says in a tired voice.

"Where's that?" I say.

"A long way from here," she says. Jane is not in a talkative mood.

I trudge up the steps. They've moved wardrobe to inside the casting building, so I pick up my stuff there. Today I'm supposed to be a regular colonist, not an aristocrat. But my clothes are just the same.

However Suzie, one of the sexy wardrobe women, stops me on my way to the make-up tent and removes my velvet hat. These make-up and wardrobe people feel they can walk up to you at any time of day or night and start fiddling with your belt, your lapels, or dabbing at your eye sockets. She's a Brit. "You aren't supposed to be quite so smart today," she says. "I'll need the vest back too."

"Are you sure?" I say. Sure enough—in the make-up tent I receive an extra coating of dirt. They discuss whether I'll need a wig, but after putting a lot of dirt and peach gel into my hair and messing it around, they decide I look authentic and disheveled enough. While I'm waiting, the hair people try to persuade one poor sot to let them cut swatches out of his hair to indicate a lice infection, but he refuses. I'm thankful they didn't try that with me.

After make-up, we extras sit and squat about outside the casting building and wait for something to happen. Most everyone but the cabin boys and I smokes while waiting, even the Indians.

My fellow extras—though all males—are a diverse lot. One is a sculptor, one is a realtor. Another is a retired fireman, another is a college dropout, and another is a used car salesman. One is an historian for a state agency, but he hasn't shown up after the first day. The others tend toward lower paying jobs or unemployment or self-employment and a minimum of education is my guess—otherwise they wouldn't be out here on a summer day with time on their hands, hair down to their shoulders, and a willingness to work for minimum wage.

Many of them try to hustle the professional women on the crew with a persistence and a crudeness that, in the academic setting that I'm familiar with, would get them thrown out on their ears or into litigation so fast they wouldn't know what hit them. Is this the way the rest of humanity behaves? I ask myself. This flagrantly? I guess so.

Would any of these accomplished and relatively beautiful young women on the crew give even a passing notice to a single one of these clueless guys. Not a chance! But the men go after it anyway.

The other side of the equation is equally amazing to me—the way the women react to their clumsy advances. The women have a way of expressing by a shrug or an inclination of their noses or a simple phrase that they could not be less interested, and it stops the men cold. Not only that, they don't lose face or the ability to keep on working with the same men. It's no big deal—either way. They keep a jaunty working relationship. What a clever way to resolve the oldest and most vexing of gender issues.

I see my pal Randy, who was also a Jamestown elder the other day. Someone told me that the next day they wanted Randy to pretend to be a chicken thief who gets shot, but he declined. Randy is a retired fireman from Newport News—I guess he thought it was beneath his dignity. "I heard they tried to kill you off," I say.

"They tried, but they couldn't do it," Randy says. "I just keep coming back for more." Randy has a great face—something you might see on an ancient coin. He says he has a heart condition and had by-pass surgery last year but—inhaling deeply on his lighted cigarette—he just can't kick the smoking habit. He thinks it may be the death of him. I nod in agreement. Randy introduces me to his brother, who is a short man with a huge beard and a deep bass voice. The brother holds his cigarette between his lips while we shake hands, then squints at me sideways to avoid the cloud of smoke he expels.

Some of the talk is about the big battle scene coming up. Four or five days of filming, and some of the colonists are already training on the muskets. Randy is one of them, and his brother is another. No one has thought to invite me yet, but for some reason as soon as I hear about it I want to be in that battle. The more I think about it, the more I like the idea. If I perform well enough, maybe they will invite me back to try and save the fort.

One of my favorite memories of early boyhood is cowboys and Indians—sometimes I was a cowboy and sometimes an Indian—and I had always enjoyed dying dramatically, pretending to be shot at the top of a hill and rolling all the way to the bottom in an agony of death throes. It was never easy to bring me down. It might take a dozen arrows. But I do know how to die. I remind myself that I need to avoid antagonizing Shirelle or flipping out again if I expect to be invited back. *What was I thinking!*

After an interminable wait while I wonder why I got up so early, we are loaded into a stake-bed truck and trundled out to a different dirt road and transported to a dock on the Chickahominy.

The heavy rains had flooded the roads out to the fort, so we have to go there and back by pontoon boat—another surprise. Nevertheless, it is a real pleasure cruising up the Chickahominy River first thing in the morning with the wind blowing our hair and the sun hot on our faces, even if we are caked with dirt.

We are told that today's shooting will involve a series of vignettes of the early colonists working to build their camp. There is no sign of the director or major actors, but the place is crawling with production assistants (PAs) and crew and extras. One of the PAs, an attractive Asian woman named Gail, selects volunteers to work on the wall of the fort, and I am one of them. Two or three other PAs are consulting about the shot and arguing about what to do. Finally, after a couple of false starts, they work it out. Something tells me these guys haven't directed anyone since film school. Their directions are a little shaky and confusing. They can't decide what they want.

Four hearty guys are to tote one of the large logs from a pile over to the high fort wall, where a trench has been dug next to the wall of logs that is already there. Four more of us await the log, which is about twenty-five feet long and nearly as large as a telephone pole, and when it arrives, we guide the stump end of it into the slot and put our backs into it to lift it in place next to the others, being sure to dodge the horizontal stake that is roped at eye level to serve as reinforcement. Then the new log is lashed into place, and another one is carried over, and the process is repeated all over again and all of our struggles are captured on celluloid.

We are not wearing gloves, of course, since we are all hard-bitten pioneers, but the logs are still bark-covered and full of sharp points where branches have been cleaved off. We cannot stand too close to the trench when the big log comes at us either because then the edges will cave in, but, unfortunately, it is difficult to gain any leverage for wrestling the log without standing precisely where we shouldn't.

Several times as I bend and stagger and push with all my might on the incoming log, I find myself within an inch or two of stabbing out my left eye on the anchor stake. Whew—this is hard work, and we are all sweating like pigs and the smoke from one of the campfires is blowing our way too and choking us.

Now three PAs are consulting again about the shot. They want us to unlash and remove the last log we just put in and carry it back to the pile and then start over—pick it up and tote it all the way back and put it into the same hole again. Don't ask me why. We do it. Then again. Then again. Then again—each effort taking much too long, I think. Surely this won't even be in the film! Must be the angle they want or the background or the light. If we keep putting in new logs, we will move farther down the field and change the angle. We try to accommodate to their wishes, but each time is such a staggering, gut-busting effort—and pulling the log out is even worse—that we begin to feel that maybe they are just torturing us for their pleasure—because they can. Probably they are just insecure about the shot and want to make sure they have it right. Finally, a break is called for, and we are finished with the fort wall.

One of the armored fellows has laid his halberd or pike on the ground and walked away with his cigarette, and now I get a good look it. What an instrument! It is essentially a battle ax mounted on the end of a long spear. Opposite the ax end is a hook-like blade for cutting the reins of a horse or jabbing at the rider or pulling him to the ground, and the spear point is razor-sharp—mounted on the end of an eight-foot pole. I've read that these weapons could take off a man's arm with a single swift blow, and they could penetrate armor. After checking it out, I give it a wide berth. A weapon this lethal should not be lying around, unattended, in my opinion.

Today, I notice that my friend Jane is a member of the water crew, passing out bottled water. I wonder if this job switch is the result of a falling out with Shirelle, or if Jane is simply trying out a different niche. She does not look at all happy. Another new person with the water crew is a large handsome fellow in a UVA ball cap. He has biceps as big as melons, and he is carrying an enormous tray filled with water bottles as if it is a mere trifle. Then there is also a young woman with dark hair and glasses who is passing out the water as if the job is beneath her.

Jane hands me a bottle and then one to Jerry, another extra who is a realtor in real life. Jerry says, "I had a dream about you last night, Jane. You and I were floating out on the river, and you didn't have any clothes on!"

Jane doesn't bat an eyelash. She says: "What a nightmare! I'm not even going to give that a moment's thought because I don't want it to stick in my mind!"

Jerry chuckles as if he knows she is just flirting with him.

6

After the break, we are part of an enormous effort to trim the fennel. Fennel is the name for the tall, fern-like plants that fill the field and surround the encampment. We wouldn't want the Indians to sneak up on us through the fennel and zap us in our sleep, so we have to trim it. An enormous ramp-and-platform has been erected so that the cameraman can pan above our heads and take in the full expanse of the meadow.

The prop guy dumps out a bag of sickles and blades with handles, and then an old man in a large straw hat who looks exactly like a cagey old farmer out of Central Casting takes over.

He is the Vegetation and Gardening Specialist. He gives us a little demonstration of how we are supposed to use the implements, and he is determined that we do it correctly. Each of us cuts a few sprigs of fennel to see how it feels and to see if we pass muster. Several of my colleagues need additional instruction. Then the PAs position us at strategic locations throughout the field of fennel, while the cameraman tries to find the right angle from his platform.

A long delay follows while a large woman in a cowboy hat, who Randy says is the assistant producer, argues with the Vegetation and Gardening Specialist about how much fennel we are to cut. She is afraid we will denude the field in a short time and that they might need the fennel to be upright for later scenes. She thinks we should, therefore, just pretend to cut the fennel but not actually cut any.

The Vegetation and Gardening Specialist is appalled by this idea. He thinks she is intruding into his area of expertise, and he thinks her idea is outrageous. From his point of view, there is enough fennel here to sink several battleships. She insists she has to keep the big picture in mind. It will look hokey, he says, if we just pretend to cut the fennel. He wants to see the real thing with a lot of thrashing arms and great bundles of cut fennel carried about. He has a vision of how it should look! It's his job to make it look authentic, and, by God, he wants to do his job!

When these creative differences are resolved, we are instructed to cut "a little" fennel but not very much! Mainly we are to just whack away and look like we are cutting more than we really are. If we do accidentally cut any fennel, we are to hold it in a clump in one hand and pretend to cut the same fennel over and over again with the other. Finally we are unleashed with our implements and the camera is rolling, rolling, rolling, but it is not easy to *not* cut the fennel—but to look as if we are. "This is hard work," I say to Randy, between swings.

"This is *acting*," Randy mumbles.

Next we do a short scene where Argall (Yorick Van Wageningen) breaks up a fight between the colonists. Yorick has suddenly appeared in his chair, but he appears to be asleep. (The real actors have their own chairs with their names on the canvas backs, just like in the movies.) Poor Yorick. Given the percentage of available hunks (of which he is one of the few) to nubile young women here, he is seriously outnumbered; and one can only imagine what his evenings must be like. He doesn't look as if he slept a wink all night.

The fight begins, and the rest of us gather around to watch it. Instead of trying to stop the mayhem, we cheer the combatants and urge them on. We do several takes on this in order to rev ourselves up to the necessary pitch of bloodthirstiness before the camera and Yorick are required. Finally we have it down pat, and at the appointed moment, Yorick suddenly appears (wide awake) to step in and do the civilized thing. Very little is required of him in the scene—he brings all that is necessary and then disappears for the day.

Our next assignment is to hoe the garden plot, and I have been selected as one of the front-row hoers because the Vegetation and Gardening Specialist likes the way I swing my implement. This hoe is not an ordinary hoe but a primitive forerunner of the hoe we know as a hoe. It has a thick, heavy wooden handle and an oversized wooden blade, and it takes more than the usual strength and determination to raise it to shoulder level and come down hard to break up the clods the way the Vegetation and Gardening Specialist wants us to do.

The person directing us now is an actor named Ben Mendelsohn, an Australian. I had my doubts about Ben a few days earlier when I was a Jamestown elder because he was so irrepressible that he was jabbering with Yorick in German and making probably lewd jokes under his breath, and my spotty college German was too lame to pick up what they were laughing about.

But Ben is so much a better director than the PAs who had preceded him that I decide I might need to revise my opinion about him. He is loud and clear and in your face, and he knows exactly what he wants; and from the point of view of the actor being directed, that's at least half the battle.

Ben's mind is teeming with language so that now he is making his lewd, rude, and crude jokes in English (with an Australian accent) right along with his direction. He is brilliant, but with his obscene imagination, Ben wouldn't last five minutes in a college classroom—the thought police would haul him off to jail. But very quickly Ben has us doing a complex scene with hoers hoeing, chickens scratching in the dirt, carriers trotting by with loads of cut fennel in their grasp; and then an ugly confrontation develops between one scraggly-looking hoer and a short innocent-looking one.

During break, one of the make-up women comes along and holds up a can, which is the signal to close your eyes. She squirts my face with a cool mist. "What's that?" I say.

"Sweat," she says. Then she pulls out a small camera and hands it to a smiling young woman with wispy blond hair, who snaps my picture.

"What's that for?" I say.

"Continuity," she says and smiles again, as if she has just said something very witty.

"The colonists are getting irritable with one another," Ben says, "and this scene just reveals the beginning of their bleeping misery. They thought they were going to find bleeping gold here, and instead they found scurvy, malnutrition, mosquitoes, and typhoid. The sun is beating down. They're hungry and dirty and pissed off." Ben shows the scraggly hoer how he wants him to shove the little guy in the chest and knock him down in the middle of the garden. The scraggly hoer, who is more timid than he appears, has a difficult time finding the necessary vehemence at first, but after several short lessons from Ben he is the absolute picture of vindictiveness. Cameras roll. My job is to hoe right along until I hear the scuffling behind me and then to turn around in astonishment.

In the heat of the day, I look around me at my fellow extras and suddenly realize they are a striking lot. There is not an ordinary-looking fellow in the group. I realize there is an extraordinary talent for physiognomy behind these choices. What I can possibly bring to the table in this regard is beyond me. But I guess I must seem as odd-looking to the casting people as this bizarre collection of memorable beards and sharp noses and aggressive brows surrounding me. I guess that is a good thing, though maybe I am simply more odd-looking than I ever realized before.

7

Speaking of hungry colonists, I am starting to feel pretty bleeping hungry myself, and it's not just the role I'm taking on. I haven't eaten anything since 5 A.M., and it's almost three in the afternoon by now.

Finally, lunch break is called, and we see that the pontoon boats are moving in towards shore, so we start to amble in that direction. Several of our number wade out to the first boat and throw down a gangplank and start to load the women and children first. But then the mistress of the crew shows up and insists that all members of the crew must go first! She even forces the little cabin boys and their mothers to get out to make way for the crew. The crew takes all the seats in all the pontoon boats, so those of us who are among the rabble or are ten-year-old cabin boys or their mothers have to wait until the boats go all the way down river to the dock and unload the crew and then come back for us.

While all this is going down, I notice that the young photographer with wispy hair who had snapped my picture earlier is one of the crew members waiting to board. "Is there any chance of getting a copy of that picture you took of me?" I say. "I just want it for posterity."

"Shhhh," she says.

"Oh, that's a taboo subject?" I say.

"Kind of, yeah," she says, breathlessly, glancing around to see if anyone is watching us. "If they ever found out, I'd be in trouble for sure." She grins and rolls her eyes in a way that indicates she's willing to do it anyway.

"Okay," I say, "forget it then. I don't want to get you in any trouble."

"I'll probably get in trouble just for talking to you."

"I'll stop talking if you want me to."

"Could we keep it on the DL?"

"The DL?" (In the world I inhabit, the DL is the Disabled List.)

"The Down Low."

"The Down Low—okay. Sure. I won't tell a soul. You can trust me on that."

"It's digital," she says. "I'll make you a copy on my computer tonight and bring it back tomorrow."

"That's awfully nice of you," I say. "I'll reimburse you for it."

"No way," she says. "It's free, and it's *special delivery*. That'll be my good deed for the day." She smiles at me out of the corners of her eyes, holds it for an instant, then flips her hair, turns, and ambles slowly away towards the waiting boat.

When we finally get back to base camp and file into the casting building, we see that members of the crew are already eating comfortably in a room with long tables that is especially set aside for them, but because Wardrobe has moved into the building and usurped a good deal of space we must eat off our laps on a few folding chairs in one of the crowded side rooms or sitting on the floor in the hall. At least we are permitted to eat what is left of lunch in the same cafeteria line where the crew preceded us, and it looks to be a full meal of fried chicken or ribs (I choose some of both), ample vegetables and salad, and a selection of desserts (I decide to sample no more than three, which is three more than I usually eat for lunch).

I sit with a bunch of other extras in one of the side rooms, jammed together with our knees hunched up between the folding chairs. One of them is a short, talkative fellow with a gigantic beard who resembles Robinson Crusoe. At first I think it is Randy's brother, who resembles him; but quickly I realize this is another guy named Michener. Michener says he is a sculptor, but every member of his family, including his father, is a scientist of one kind or another. He says he probably should have become a scientist too, but it didn't work out. All this is a preliminary to his main story, which is that *under no circumstances* should any of us set foot into the Chickahominy River!

"They may ask you to go into the river today," he says. "But don't do it unless you wear a condom!" My first impression of Michener is that the poor fellow is off his rocker.

"My father is a world-renowned bacteriologist," he says. "He knows what he's talking about, and when I told him we were filming near the river, he said, 'Son, there are dangerous flesh-eating amoebas in the Chickahominy that will eat your penis off! They can infect any open wound or enter your body through any open orifice. Don't go near the water!' I said, "Dad, this is no joking matter. I'm surprised at you,' and he said, 'Son, I would never joke about a thing like this. I'm telling you—*don't* go into that river or you may regret it the rest of your life!"

Several of the other extras shoot questions at Michener, and Michener has good answers. I decide he may not be so crazy after all. Michener confides to us that he has brought his own condom—in case of an emergency. Jerry the realtor asks if he has any extras, and Michener says no. Then Jerry says he has an emergency too—he was just thinking of fucking one of the make-up women after lunch, and everyone laughs.

Michener and most of the others finish and wander away, and one of the cabin boys sits down next to me on one of the folding chairs. After eating in silence for several minutes, he says bitterly, "Why does the crew get to eat in *there*, and we have to eat in *here*? Why does the crew always get to go first?"

"Because they are *professionals*," I say, "and we aren't. They are members of a Union, and we aren't. We are just here for this movie, but the crew will be here for the next movie too—the movie company needs them more than it needs us. So it has to treat them better."

"At least they could be polite about it," he says.

Joe David Bellamy

8

As we ride back toward the dock, I can see the other fort-set in the distance across a wide field of fennel. This is an entirely different set and location from the one where we are supposed to be building the fort. That is, this is supposed to be the fort we are building but at a much later stage of development—already finished and lived in, for a time. According to an article in *The Virginian-Pilot*, more than forty local carpenters helped build the set a few months ago, but it is so rough-hewn and weathered-looking, it might have been there for fifty years. I desperately want to see it up close—it is one beautiful fort. It is probably the fort where the big battle scene will take place.

Back at our half-built fort after lunch, we are preparing for a scene where a small boat called a shallop is being unloaded. I can't believe it! They are going to put us all in the river! I have to find some way to get out of it!

The shallop has just sailed in from the mother ship and is full of stuff. The scene requires quite a bit of preparation. First, the prop people bring over an assortment of boxes and barrels and crates of several sizes and amphora and coils of giant nautical ropes and wicker baskets and leather pouches. Terrence Malick, our director, and Joerg, the chief cameraman, and their immediate crew are bustling about on a little cliff above the beach gazing out across the water at the mother ship and at the shallop and the accumulation of cargo-like items.

Mr. Malick is scouting out camera angles by peering at the scene through a window made by holding up his extended fingers like a camera lens and then discussing what he wants with Joerg, and some of the carpenters are making wooden pegs out of skinned tree limbs to plug the spout-holes in the barrels, then pounding them in with wooden mallets. The campfires are swirling, sending smoke in all directions; and a couple of dogs are wandering around looking for a handout.

We begin by forming a line along the beach and passing the barrels and boxes and crates and rope and amphora and pouches out to the men in the water, who load them aboard the shallop. I have accidentally-on-purpose ended up at the end of the line above the beach near and mostly underneath the outstretched branches of a big tree, the last person in the line, and the farthest from the water with its dreaded amoebas. So when the barrels and boxes and crates and rope and amphora and pouches come back along the line, as we are unloading them, I have to navigate several root systems at my feet to jockey my cargo up to the flat area to put it down—otherwise it will roll down the hill into the water.

Some of the barrels are small enough to carry, but the big ones are full-sized wooden barrels with iron barrel staves and too heavy to move except by rolling them up the incline over the roots, then twisting them upright to sit on their circular ends. Some of the crates are large enough to require a party of two to move them.

If I do not move much faster than normal, the cargo begins to pile up at the bank, and the whole line grinds to a standstill because of me. The director keeps yelling at us to hurry up, we're moving too slowly. Apparently no one in command seems to realize the nature of the problem, but I begin to feel like a man in a Charlie Chaplin film, working at double-time and still overwhelmed at the end of the assembly line.

Then I begin to notice several large bees darting loudly over my head like B-52s. One of the bearded extras who looks like Robinson Crusoe—sure enough, it's Michener—points to the tree where PA Shirelle is hiding and informs us all, in a loud voice, that the nest is in *that* tree and that those "bees" are, in fact, highly dangerous Japanese hornets and their sting can be deadly. If we don't bother them, they won't bother us, he says, but don't do anything crazy!

But what might the hornets regard as crazy? They have been out here for maybe fifty years with no one to bother them, and all of a sudden they have a New Line Cinema production of *The New World* at their doorstep and a bunch of nuts lugging barrels. PA Shirelle, who is a black woman from the Bronx, decides to find a new hiding place, but my post is immediately adjacent to the hornet tree, so I have no choice but to continue to ply my barrels in their vicinity or to risk a watery death by amoeba.

It takes an enormous effort to unload the whole batch of cargo and pass it along the beach and up to its resting place on the shore, and once we start rolling, the Animal Specialist brings out two live pigs about the size of Dalmatians that we are supposed to be unloading also. However, when the pigs are passed out over the water, they think they are about to be drowned and they start to scream and thrash about in such a desperate, comical way that I can't help laughing as soon as I hear it and see it. I wonder if the hornets will regard this as a provocation? The noise the pigs make is deafening, even from my distant vantage point; and the handlers are having a hard time controlling their charges. It is impossible to pass them along from hand-to-hand without actually drowning them. So one strong-armed fellow is elected to carry them over and back a couple of times for the benefit of the camera, and then the pigs are retired.

At the break, Shirelle yells for someone to come and spray this bleeping hornet's nest with some insect repellent. Shirelle barks the command into her walkie-talkie, but Michener runs up to her and explains that that would be the *worst possible thing to do*. He gestures wildly. She absolutely *must not* do that or he for one will not be responsible for the outcome. "The hornets will fly out in a swarm and everyone will be stung to death!" he yells. "Don't do it!" Who is this Michener guy? Well, he is the son of a famous bacteriologist! Shirelle doesn't know that but is persuaded to cool it. We will just have to live with the hornets.

Once we have unloaded all the cargo and I have carried each item up the hill and placed it on the flat area while deadly hornets are buzzing overhead, we have to do another take, which means passing all the cargo back the way it came and doing the whole thing over again. But as the afternoon wears along and the light shifts and the camera angles are multiplied, the tide starts to come in so that the workers who were originally walking their heavy loads along the sandy shore are starting to stagger ankle-deep in the waters of the Chickahominy, then knee-deep, then waist-deep.

I hope, for their sakes, that Michener's father was wrong about the dreaded amoebas in the water. I have managed to stay on dry land myself, just in case. I know this much—the gear is getting wet as they float it across, and their shoes are hopeless. My position on top of the bank now seems like a very lucky move, and I am determined to keep my feet (and everything above my knees) dry as long as possible.

But for take after take, there is much more sogginess to deal with. The barrels are slick from the drenching they are taking, and the plugs are failing. So each time the barrels return, they are slippery and sloshing with water inside and heavier than before. My hands are numb, but I keep lifting and bending and pushing the barrels up the hill in hopes that I am impressing Shirelle.

Terrence Malick is a perfectionist and is apparently famous for the number of takes he does for each scene, and he is also famous for loving twilight. So now that a hint of darkness is in the air, he is in some kind of movie-making heaven while we bend our backs like slaves to please him. At least the hornets seem to have dozed off for the night.

Then our director decides that he would like to shoot the whole scene from the water, so our pal Ben Mendlesohn, the Aussie actor, who seems to have evolved into an assistant director, is appointed to oversee our labor; and Malick and crew disappear toward the mother ship on a pontoon boat. Ben immediately gets into the spirit of his role by pretending he is the wicked overseer. "All right, you lazy sots," he yells, "you good-for-nothing rats! Bring it in! Haul dem barrels, you fools! Come on! What are you waiting for? We haven't got all day here! Move it or else!"

Shirelle, who is in contact with Malick and crew on her walkie-talkie, forwards instructions from the distant pontoon boat. Every time we hear the dreaded "Reset!" from Shirelle, we know we have to pass the cargo back again; and every time we finish unloading the cargo, we hope against hope that this will be the last time, and then Shirelle croaks, "Reset!" again and Ben starts in on us.

"All right, you limeys!" he yells. "All right, you stubborn lunkheads! Let's see some work here or I'll put the whip to ya! Let's see some real muscle here! Let's see some hard work! I know you're good for it! Come on, rats! Come on, you dirty rats! Muscle up!"

Then Shirelle calls out "Reset," and we have to start all over again. Now it is almost dark! "All right, you dirty rascals!

You miserable low-lifes! You stubborn dim-witted fools! Bring in the gear! Bring it in now!"

Someone gazes out across the water and points out that Malick and crew are shooting towards the ship. They are not even pointing in our direction. It turns out someone across the water has forgotten to notify Shirelle that they are done with us. Shirelle hears "rolling, rolling, rolling" on her walkie-talkie and thinks they mean us. But they don't!

As soon as Ben realizes what has happened, he explodes: "Listen to me, these lads have worked their hearts out here today, and they are *tired*! If you are not even going to be filming over here, let us know! What a bunch of bullshit! Blast it! These men have set a standard of hard work that you should try to emulate, you bleeping idiots. By God, these men deserve better!"

Spontaneous applause erupts from the extras in the water and on shore—and from me. Now Ben is our hero. We are finished for the day! And, thank God, I still have all my appendages!

Joe David Bellamy

9

Every night when I come home from the set, starving and exhausted, it takes me an hour or more to get the make-up off, using mainly a combination of cold cream and rubbing alcohol. I also try hydrogen peroxide, soap, and shampoo, and even briefly consider Clorox. I line up the chemicals, the cotton swabs, the washrags and paper towels on top of the lavatory and, squinting and rubbing, glare at myself with tired eyes in the mirror as I try to return to normal. The transition is startling—I start with the face of a glamorous thug and end up with that of a pale older man I'm not certain I recognize.

Even then, after all the rubbing that leaves my skin raw in some places, the grime isn't entirely gone. Some days I wonder if I will ever be clean again. The artificial dirt sinks into the pores of my neck and shoulders and in the wings of my nose like a dye, but it looks like the real thing. Then, after I've scrubbed as much as I dare, I crawl into the shower and use more soap and shampoo in heavy doses. Nevertheless, in spite of this miserable ritual, whenever Jeannie or her assistant calls again, I drop everything, set the alarm for four o'clock in the morning, and go back for another coating of fresh and nearly indelible filth, grease, and color. Why do I do it?

Several days pass and then Jeannie calls to ask if I can come in the next day early? I say sure. She says I'll be playing a colonist who is a sentinel and who falls asleep on the job and then the Indians show up. Something tells me I'm going to get my throat cut and it won't be pretty, but it's all in a good cause. This could be my big moment! It does mean getting up at 4 A.M., but for this kind of opportunity some sacrifice should be expected.

When I reach *The New World* base camp, it's barely daylight and the make-up tent is crawling with Indians. The Indians are getting sprayed from top to bottom to make them redder, and that's just the beginning. It's a huge job to get them ready—several coats of make-up and elaborate hair-dos—and the Indians are scary as hell in their make-up and war paint. Several of them are very tall and muscular, and they have stern expressions on their faces and, of course, knives and hatchets, not to mention feathers.

They are also nearly naked. In some cases, their loincloths don't quite cover their nether regions, but they don't seem to care. It goes with being an Indian, they seem to feel, though some of them are actually Latinos. Every once in a while, when you walk by one of them near the tent or in the casting building, the stern expression suddenly changes and he says, "S'up, man," or "How's it goin'?"

There are only two other colonists today, and we have to wait until the Indians are finished before getting our gel and lather of expensive dirt. So we are just sitting there, sweating, watching the process. The sun is beating down this morning—the temperature is already in the low nineties—and even with several large fans inside the tent, the heat is overwhelming. Suddenly the head make-up guy yells over to the main hair lady, "I've called twice now for more bottled water, and it's still not here! If it's not here in two minutes, I'm walking straight out of here! Will you bring your girls and join me?"

The hair woman hesitates. Obviously she doesn't like the idea. Before she can reply, the make-up guy throws his sponge and screams, "Thanks so much for supporting me!" and runs out of the tent, and the rest of his staff follows. The hair woman shakes her head wearily, then summons her girls and walks out as well, leaving behind a group of half-finished Indians. Five minutes later they are all back at work, we are all drinking from our bottles of water, every station has several bottles of water immediately at hand, except the make-up guy has a whole case of his own.

Outside, I look around for the cute photo-girl who might have my picture ready, but she is nowhere to be found. I start talking to a white-haired man dressed in civilian clothes. It turns out he is the dialogue coach for the Indians. He is a professor at the University of North Carolina at Charlotte, and he is one of two people in North America who knows the Algonquin language and how it should sound when spoken aloud. The Indians in the film will be speaking their dialogue in the original tongue of Powhatan's tribe, he says, and their lines will all have English subtitles!

One of the serious problems the colonists faced, he says, is that they couldn't understand what the Indians were saying. So Terrence Malick wants to dramatize that facet of the overall plight for both groups. I get the idea this is going to be an unusual film that attempts to tell the Jamestown story from a culturally unbiased perspective, if such a thing is possible, or possibly even from the point of view of the Indians. It occurs to me that this film may indeed be worth getting up at four in the morning for and then spending several hours in a hot tent! I hope it is. I wouldn't want to be immortalized as part of a movie that bombed. But that's the chance you take, right?

    Gradually the Indians disappear, and it is our turn in make-up. My fellow throat-cut victim in the scene we are about to do is a skinny red-headed young man named Timothy. When we are ready to go, Timothy and I and another guy named Greg ride to the Indian camp in a van.

    Greg says he was out here yesterday all day shooting a scene where he was dressed in armor and standing in a hole by the river. He was told the scene is supposed to be Powhatan's dream of an armored Englishman rising out of the sea. It was hell to shoot but should be interesting to see on film, Greg concludes. "That bleeping armor is hot," he says, "especially with the sun beating down."

    I find a rolled up section of the day's script pressed into the crease of the seat. Someone has thrown it away or forgotten it. I guess the real actors have the opportunity to orient themselves to each day's shoot by means of such crib sheets. The extras do not, which possibly explains why we feel disoriented.

    I ask Greg about the rumor that the Chickahominy is infested with flesh-eating amoebas or bacteria, and he says he doesn't know about that. But what he does know is that one of the extras who was toting barrels from the shallop the other day got an infection or some damned thing in his leg and it swelled up to three times normal size.

    "What did they do with him?" I say in astonishment.

    "They rushed him to the hospital and pumped him full of antibiotics and saved his life. That's what I heard anyway," Greg says.

    "My god," Timothy says. "Don't go in the water!"

    "Right," I say, and then I tell them everything Michener told us.

When the van stops, we get out and follow several snakes of cables into the deep forest, where we come upon a huge wigwam or longhouse about half the size of a football field and maybe three stories high. The structure is made entirely out of saplings tied together with rawhide and then covered with suede-colored skins, except the very top, at the back, where some green and purple tarps had been thrown on the roof. (I presume that is okay because it is out of camera range.)

This wigwam is so large that while Malick and camera crew are shooting the scene in front of it, the extras and make-up and wardrobe women and the Water crew and the Food crew and all the rest of the crew and the mothers and fathers of the children pretending to be Indians are camping out behind it, completely out of sight.

Timothy and I are greeted by Alex, who says she will be looking after us today. She is a personable young British woman with a blond ponytail, and the first thing she wants to do is dab us with a little bit more dirt from her make-up rag. We are accustomed to the drill by now, so we stand patiently while she pats us, giving special attention to necks, elbows, knees, and my shoes, which are still too new-looking in spite of everyone's efforts to ruin them. Then she shows us the food tent and tells us to just take it easy in this vicinity. "They'll call you when they're ready," she says, "but, frankly, I doubt if they'll get to that scene this morning."

Timothy and I find a couple of unoccupied golf carts with canopies, where we can sit and take off our heavy sword belts. I eat an apple and occupy myself with people-watching, while Timothy finds a way to lie down in his golf cart and promptly falls asleep.

Some kind of big Indian confab is going on beyond the giant wigwam with drum-beating and war whoops, and occasionally Terrence Malick's voice may be heard on a bullhorn, exhorting them to even greater levels of frenzy. Some wardrobe women have a tent to my left where they are sewing feverishly, and one of the dads is trying to impress one of the moms by telling her in excruciating detail about a construction project he was a part of. "Then they brought in this girder that was *seventy feet long* and lowered it into place!" The mom is desperately bored, but she is kindly pretending to be interested in the nuts and the bolts and even in the girders.

I walk around a little and am startled behind one tent by a full-grown deer, still unskinned, hanging upside down by its feet. On closer inspection, it is not a real deer, but you'd never know it from three feet away. I walk over by the edge of the wigwam to examine the mayhem out front. It seems to be a war dance, and the Indians are mad as hell. I search for the cute photographer, but apparently she is not here today. I hope she didn't get in trouble by talking to me and promising the photo.

Two men approach me with a little girl, and one of the men says to me, "Would you kindly say hello to my niece. Honey, I'd like to introduce you to Mr. Plummer. We met you down at Telluride, you may recall." The little girl smiles and puts her hand out towards me.

"I'm afraid you've mistaken me for someone else," I say. "But I would be happy to say hello to such a charming girl anyway," I say, bending down to shake her hand. "I don't think Mr. Plummer is here today actually," I say, "but I'm sure he would have been delighted to meet you." They all smile politely as if they are every bit as pleased to meet me as they would have been to meet the great actor himself. Such is the power of costume and make-up and a good leather belt.

I wander back to my golf cart, where Alex informs me that nothing is happening with our scene, just as she suspected. "Maybe after lunch," she says cheerily.

A dark-haired young woman wearing thick glasses sits down on the edge of my golf cart. "Is it okay if I sit here for a while?" she asks.

"Sure," I say. With that, she slides in and collapses with a sigh. I tell her we are waiting for the Indians to finish so that we can do our thing.

"Oh," she says, clearly not interested.

"What's your role?" I ask.

"I was hired to be a member of the crew—to serve water—but Monday the Union got involved and now I'm not allowed to do anything. Several of us were fired." *I wonder if Jane was one of the people involved in this purge? I haven't seen her.*

"You don't belong?"

"No. Heavens no. I graduated from William and Mary in June, and now I'm doing this. I thought I might go to LA, but I was hoping to make some connections here." She has a frustrated, petulant look about her, a thoroughly disgruntled look.

"I think I saw you with the water crew last week," I say.

"I was doing a really good job! I was very conscientious. It's really such a shame. I've just been coming in every day anyway, just wondering around. But I feel like such a fool."

"Does anyone know you're still here?" She doesn't meet my eyes but looks off into the sewing tent.

"I'm not sure. I should write a note to Terry, I think, and tell him what happened to me," she says. "Don't you think?"

"Terrence *Malick*, you mean?" If she's on a first name basis with Malick, what's her problem, I wonder?

"Terry, yes," she says, as if he's an old family friend.

"It might be worth a try," I say. "What kind of work were you hoping to do in LA then—production stuff?"

"I don't know," she says. "I doubt it…no. Acting…. But you have to find some way to get your foot in the door." She takes her glasses off and gives me a long look at her profile. She has a huge mane of striking black hair, but her nose is too long and she looks far too nerdy to be anything but a character actress. Of course, I keep all that to myself.

It's not as if I am any sort of talent agent, after all, but I think of the long line of hopeful young women—some of them quite beautiful—who showed up for the casting call in Charles City County and who probably waited eagerly by the phone for weeks afterwards for a call that never came. Most of them wanted to change their lives. Any of them would have been happy to do what I am doing, but, unfortunately, this film does not have many roles for young women. It's all Pocahontas—all the time. I wonder if any of them realizes that?

Finally, our lunch call comes, and I wish her luck. "I would definitely contact Malick," I say. "He might be able to find something for you—surely. And if he can't or won't, no harm done."

"Right, thanks," she says, a little sarcastically, as if she has already been over this same ground a hundred times and doesn't need my advice. Well, she did ask!

10

Back at base camp, Shirelle buttonholes Timothy and me and escorts us into the cafeteria line. "You guys are scheduled for right after lunch," she says. "So I want you to be ready to roll, okay?"

"Sure thing," I say. Shirelle forces us to the head of the line, bypassing several hungry-looking members of the crew who are starting to collect outside the cafeteria building, then she disappears. But just as Timothy and I are scooping food onto our plates, the female crew chief shows up, the same one who had thrown the mothers and kids off the pontoon boats.

"What are *you* doing here?" she says. "The crew eats first."

"I know," I say, "but Shirelle wanted us to start early because we have a scene right after lunch."

"Tough," she says. "You can't eat until the crew is done." My salivary glands are already cutting loose. For a long moment I stare into her rigid face, thinking I might just keep on walking down the line, shoveling food onto my plate to see what she will do. But I decide against it. She is probably Shirelle's boss.

"Fine," I say.

We slouch our way toward the empty end of the room, and I take off my sword and throw it on the table, where it thumps and clatters loudly. Several crew members turn to see what is going on. I remind myself that this is no time to flip out if I want to impress Shirelle and make it to the battle scene.

"That was totally uncalled for," I say. "What a bleeping bitch." Timothy agrees. We sink into our chairs—two dirty, lonely outcasts, two beggars not permitted in the company of their betters—and watch everyone else eat. I decide I am not cut out to be a peon. My ego can't take it. I am so furious that if any Indian tries to slit my throat today, I may fight back. I may have no choice.

When we are finally permitted to get in line, an hour or so later, we have about five minutes to stuff it down before Shirelle appears. "Why are you still eating?" she snaps.

"They threw us out of line," I say. "They wouldn't let us eat until the crew was finished."

"Oh," she says. "Well, I need you in the van now."

"Here we come," I say, gnawing on my last bite and strapping on my sword.

We speed to the location, and when we get there, a place that looks like a crossroads under some tall sycamores, Shirelle hops out. We see her conferring with a couple of other PAs, then she crawls back in. "They don't need us yet," she says, "but they might need us later." So we cruise back to the base camp, which is now nearly deserted. "Wait here," Shirelle says. "I'll get back to you as soon as I know anything." She hops onto her golf cart and zips away toward the set.

We sit in a couple of aluminum deck chairs out in front of the cafeteria, just Timothy and me, and nothing happens for an hour. We watch the pine boughs waving gently in the breeze and listen to the hum of insects going about their business. Another hour passes. Obviously, Shirelle doesn't need us or has forgotten us.

Finally, I tell Timothy that I have a camera in the trunk of my car. Would he care to stroll down the road a short distance and we could take some pictures of ourselves in costume. He says he thinks that would be a great idea, so we stand up and stretch and then head out of the camp on foot and down the long rural road, flanked by giant virgin trees and fields of fennel and tall grass.

Timothy says he knows we aren't supposed to take any pictures of ourselves because the first day they told all the colonists that such picture-taking was strictly taboo, but he would definitely like to get some shots for his gymnastics group and his girlfriend. It isn't as if we are trying to sell any photos to *Entertainment Weekly*, he says. Of course not, I say, a prospect that never occurred to me. "They didn't tell me any such thing," I said. "They must have forgotten. I can't understand what the big deal is about the pictures," I say, wondering ruefully if the young woman photographer had gotten in trouble because of my request. For whatever reason, she had never returned.

"I can't either," he says. "I just hope we don't get caught."

When we arrive at my car, I pop open the trunk and remove the camera from its leather case. Timothy poses along the side of the road and I snap his picture. Then another in profile. So far, so good. Then Timothy says he wants me to try and capture him in the middle of a cartwheel—for his gymnastics group. I say I'm not certain I can do it because it's a digital camera that doesn't do motion very well but I'll try. Then Timothy does several cartwheels and handstands in the middle of the road while I make every effort to time the exposure and snap the shot at exactly the right instant. The sun is too bright to be able to examine the results, so we forge ahead, hoping for the best. Timothy returns the favor, snapping several shots of me, and then quickly I lock the camera back inside my trunk and we hike back towards camp the same way we came.

"I think we got away with it," he says.
"I think we did too. Don't tell anybody."
"I won't," he says.

Back at camp there is still nothing to do, so Timothy and I chat about his love life. He brings it up. He says he is twenty-one-years-old and a college dropout. The girl he is going out with now is driving him crazy. She is so beautiful he can't think about anything else, but some days she won't even speak to him. Other days all she wants to do is make love, which she does with great enthusiasm and abandon, but then she wants to leave right afterwards. He thinks she's just using him, that she doesn't respect him or love him the way he loves her. I agree that it sounds like a terrible problem. I advise returning to school and becoming a man of consequence as soon as possible. Women tend to respect success, I say. They're funny that way.

As twilight is falling and no one has thought to either use us or excuse us, we are still sitting in front of the aluminum casting building. Timothy gets up and walks behind one of the semi trailers, then quickly returns, all aflutter.

He says, "Oh, my god, Colin is sitting out in front of his trailer!"
"What's he doing? Just taking in the evening light?" I say.
"I guess."
"Why don't you go talk to him."
"Are you kidding? I should. I really should."
"Just pretend like you're walking by on the way to the men's room."
"I should. I'll probably never have another chance like this. My sister will kill me if I don't do it."
"Good luck then."
"Here I go."
In a few minutes he comes back.

"I did it!" he says.
"What did he say?"
"He said, 'How're ya doin?'"
"What did you say?
"I said, 'How're ya doin' right back. Oh, man, was that terrific!"
"Good for you. You think your sister will be satisfied?"
"Sure she will. That's about as good as it gets! Colin bleeping Farrell! Oh man—just think of it!"

Thus ends our day of complete futility. Always ready—never called. They also serve who only sit and wait.

11

Today we are scheduled to shoot in the built fort, but it is a very early casting call. The built fort! I get up at 4 A.M., which is four hours before my usual wake-up hour and when I hit 64 I see I have even beaten some of the hardcore Navy personnel headed for the 6 A.M. rush hour. It's *that* early, but—you'd be surprised—the Interstate is far from deserted at that hour. The long drive to *The New World* base camp is like another dream. I sleep-walk through wardrobe and hair and make-up and find myself crammed in the back of the stake-bed truck with about fifty other drowsy-looking extras, some colonists, some Indians, dodging the low-hanging tree branches and bouncing our way toward the prop van and the built fort, which we can see in the distance across a field of tassles as soon as we turn from the main access road.

At the prop van, I decide I am too tired to drag a heavy sword around all day, so I go with a medium-sized dagger, which fits comfortably on my belt. Today, I have wisely brought along some nuts and some gum in my pouch, so I am ready to face any long bouts of starvation and boredom. From the prop van, we walk the short remaining distance to the fort, which faces the Chickahominy River. I never thought I'd make it to the built fort, but here I am on this beautiful morning, exhausted but grateful to be here. My heart stirs at the sight of it, as it used to when I was twelve years old watching Randolph Scott movies.

What is it about a fort? A fort is a beautiful thing, and this one seems extraordinarily beautiful. How many times have I seen the U.S. Cavalry absolutely save the day at the end of a long battle when they show up in the nick of time, carbines blazing, at just such a fort. Well, as I walk in through the huge double log doors, I see this fort is a little more primitive than that perhaps. Randolph Scott might not have been entirely comfortable here. It is like walking back in time, and we are about two centuries from anywhere Randolph Scott would have saddled a horse.

Inside the high rough-hewn walls is an entire little village, several primitive cottages with thatched roofs, a blacksmith's layout, an old rusty cannon in the middle of the yard, pointing out toward the river, and the skeleton framework of a church with the large plank pews already in place inside. I walk in between the 2 x 4s and lie down carefully on one of the pews and gaze up at the sky through the roof joists. I am so bloody tired I can barely hold myself upright. I shut my eyes and try to relax as the crew assembles and time floats.

After a while, I lift my head. Mr. Malick is over at the other end of the camp conferring about the shoot, but several PAs have gathered in the center of the yard and are calling to us to look alive. While we are waiting for the others, I walk over towards Shirelle. She looks at me and does a double-take. "Joe, they really messed you up in make-up today. You look terrible!"

"I know. We're supposed to be starving, you know. It's not easy being a colonist, Shirelle."

"It's not easy being a PA either," she says, winking at me. Shirelle and I seem to be developing a nice rapport, and I am grateful for it because she is usually all business and one tough cookie.

The PA with the bullhorn says loudly they want us to scatter among the buildings and try to look as if we are just hanging out, so I find a stump near the center of things and pick up a stick and pretend to whittle on it. It's a perfect spot. Another PA says we are all too far to his right. He wants us all to move to his left. Reluctantly, I give up my stump and amble back toward the church. One young guy who has a talent for upstaging everyone grabs my stump, and I can't help feeling usurped. The PAs look us over, and then one walks up to the young guy and says, "The script calls for these men to be thin and wasted. I'm afraid you're too healthy-looking. For this shot, why don't you go inside and stay out of sight, okay." The PA casts his eyes over the rest of us. "You," he says, pointing at me. "You come over here and sit on this stump."

Sometimes it pays to look old and decrepit, I think. *Not very often, but once in a while, it does.*

Terrence Malick walks across the yard and checks us out. He seems deep in thought. He confers with the main group of PAs, then returns to his corner. Mr. Malick does not usually speak to us directly—except through his bullhorn. We extras are just too far down the pecking order to be addressed face to face by the director, and we understand this. "He thinks it would be better if you were inside your huts," the PA says. "Find a place inside and then you will all come out when John Smith appears at the other end of the camp." I get up and go inside the nearest hut along with three other extras and a couple of the PAs. The PAs immediately lie down on the two straw-filled beds inside, and one of them seems to fall asleep. *I would too* if I had a place to lie down. One of the extras is a tall young man I haven't seen before—in the costume of an aristocrat but without a shirt. He has a flushed face and diamond-tipped studs through his nipples. He can't stop talking in an annoying way to the one PA still awake, as if he thinks this is a job interview. I try to ignore them, but I can't help wondering why someone would voluntarily skewer himself in that way. It hurts my chest just to think about it.

Two other crew members come into the hut. One of them bends down to do something at the base of the door, and the other one starts to work on the leg of one of the beds. At first, I think they are spraying for bugs, but gradually it dawns on me that they are painting little lines everywhere they go with several different colors of paint. It's quite effective actually. They are adding authenticity by aging the wood, showing moisture lines and stress cracks. "Most of the interiors are totally bare," I hear one of them tell the PA who is still awake. "But they're going to use this one for some important scenes." The PA nods his head knowingly. On the other bed, the PA who has fallen asleep starts to wheeze and snore in a steady rhythm.

In a minute, we hear Mr. Malick on the bullhorn from his corner. "All right, colonists! John Smith has been captured by the Indians and you think he is dead! You have been here for several weeks with nothing to eat! When he suddenly appears at the door of the fort, you think he may be a ghost! You don't know whether to be grateful or fearful! Is it really him? Or have you lost your minds? All right, let's run through it a few times!" After a pregnant pause, there is movement at the back door of the fort and then the door swings open and Colin Farrell walks into the yard. We can see him through the slits between the boards in one of our windows from inside the hut. Behind him is a procession of Indians, and they have a huge deer strung up upside down from saplings they are carrying across their shoulders.

"All right, NOW!" Mr. Malick says through the bullhorn. "Come out slowly! Look him over! Is he real or is he a vision? Colin, walk a little farther in and keep moving slowly toward them.

You are a little bit shocked at the deplorable conditions in the camp." I amble out and try to look at Colin as if I am not sure he is real. He looks great actually. His clean black hair is blowing lightly in the breeze, and he is wearing a feather in it. He is strikingly handsome and graceful. He looks as if he just got back from a week in Nassau. In contrast, my colleagues look too wooden. They don't seem to know where to walk. "Let's try it again!" Mr. Malick says through his bullhorn. "Wait a little bit longer this time before you come out!"

We try this same rendition about five times without much improvement. I seem to have gotten myself closest to Colin because of the juxtaposition of our hut to the center of the yard. Before we start filming it, a crew member waters down the dirt with a green garden hose, and the animal handlers release two emaciated dogs and scatter tidbits for them in the damp yard. So the first thing Colin sees when he cracks the door of the fort is these two miserable dogs.

"Clear the set! Rolling, rolling, rolling. Action!" Mr. Malick is calling to us through the bullhorn again: "Here he comes. You thought he was dead! You can't believe your eyes. You walk towards him, but, wait, he might be a ghost!" The other extras are walking in circles like a bunch of idiots in a high school play. I can't stand to look at them. We do several takes, but it doesn't get any better. I am so bored I reach into my pouch and peel back the paper from a piece of gum and pop it into my mouth. The camera is so far away, I'm sure no one can see it.

After the last take, Colin strolls over to a spot near me and smiles in a conspiratorial way and gestures for the other extras to join us. When they are all gathered around, he says, "Look, the thing is, you see, these bleeping men have been out here in this bleeping fort for weeks without enough to eat. They are bleeping sick and in real bleeping human misery. Some of them are surely about to die. They are that close to death. They think Smith is already bleeping dead, and they are almost bloody bleeping dead themselves. They are, like, two days from thinking about bleeping eating each other. It's that bad, lads. So think about that when

Smith comes to the door, okay?" It's like a pep talk from the coach. Light bulbs seem to go off in the heads of several of my compatriots. We go back into our huts to await the next take. After a few minutes, somebody comes to our door.

"The prop guy asked me to give this to one of you in here," he says. It's a crutch." He holds it out. It is a very crudely made crutch. It looks as if it has been hewed out of a tree branch with a knife or an ax, and it is quite short, maybe four feet long. The young man with the studs in his tits has a faraway look in his eye and a contemptuous tilt to his jaw. He's obviously not interested. No one else seems to want it either, so I take it and place it under my arm and practice limping around inside the hut. I have to sag down quite a ways in order to let my weight settle into it, but I immediately feel different about myself.

In a minute or two a bald man in a blue t-shirt shows up. He wants to know who is going to use the crutch, and I say I am. He says he thinks I am too tall. I say, "No I'm not. I've been practicing it. I just have to bend into it a little bit."

"Let me see," he says. I limp a ways for him. He says, "Okay, maybe. We'll see how it goes during the shot." He ducks out. Outside they are getting ready for the next take, and somebody yells, "Clear the set!"

"Who was that guy?" I say.

"He's the Prop director," one of the PAs says.

"He seems to be taking a personal interest in my crutch."

Then I can hear the gate squeak open and through the crack in the window I see Capt. John Smith marching through with his band of Indians following and the deer strung up by its feet. My cue comes, and I stagger out of the hut and slowly clomp forward out into the middle of the clearing with my crutch, letting all my weight sag heavily into the cradle of the handle of the crutch, as if it is the only thing allowing me to walk upright. I am clearly a person in some deep agony.

I don't know how my colleagues are doing because I don't even look at them. I can see Smith, but I can't believe it's really Smith! It might be a ghost or it might even be wishful thinking on my part. By God! but I hope that deer is real because I am starving to death, and, in fact—it's about two o'clock and I haven't eaten since before five this morning—so I *am* starving to death. I stagger up to Smith, who is, of course, handsome, 28-year-old Colin Farrell with an Indian feather in his clean, hair-sprayed hair, but he has come to save us with a stuffed deer on a pole that looks real and looks like lunch, and I suddenly feel so grateful to see him that it almost makes me cry. For the first time, I have the feeling that I am really *acting*. The muscles in my face are running through a drill I have no control over, and I owe it all to my crutch.

"All right, cut! Much, much better," says Terrence Malick. "Let's do it again."

We go back into our hut. In a minute the Prop director pops in. He says: "That was terrific! You can keep using the crutch. Just keep doing it the same way."

"Okay—thanks," I say. The other extras look at me as if they are seeing me for the first time.

We do three more takes while I continue to ham it up with my crutch, and my face runs through contortions I never knew were there. I am hoping against hope that one of these scenes will make it into the movie because I would really love to see what this looks like *myself*—I know it is real because it is so weird and unconscious.

After the next take, I am still leaning on my crutch in the center of the yard when the Prop director rushes up. He says, "Are you chewing gum, by any chance?"

Oh my god, I think, *and I was trying so hard not to chew while the camera was rolling.* "Sorry," I say. "But I can lose it."

"Better lose it," he says, his face turning grim. Now I've probably ruined my all-time best performance because I was chewing gum! I guess this is what they get for $5.35/hour—a complete amateur!

12

Finally, lunch break is called. I'm in line next to Randy's big-bearded brother, trying to discreetly dodge his cigarette smoke. "Where's Randy today?" I say, trying to make conversation.

"Didn't you hear?" he says. "Randy ran a pike clean through his hand!"

"No way!"

"Yeah, he was just standing around on the set the other day, and he turned around. One of those jerks in the armor had leaned his pike over a log and just left it there, and Randy turned right into it. Didn't see it until it was clean through his hand. Bled with a stuck pig, and they had to take him to the emergency room. Those bleeping pikes are sharp as hell!"

"I know. I looked at one of them. Damn—well, that's too bad! I hope he's going to be all right."

"Yeah, he'll be all right. Randy'll be all right. Nothing stops Randy."

"You think he'll be back for the movie?"

"Well, maybe. His hand is all bandaged up right now. He's just taking it easy for a while."

"Give him my best," I say. "My name is Joe. He'll remember me."

"Sure thing, Joe. I'll tell him you asked about him."

Today the extras in my group are all aflutter with a hot rumor. An actress was needed who was willing to bare her breasts and pretend to be an Indian maiden for a particular scene at the Indian camp—not a speaking part, you understand—just a slice of authentic background—and one of our very own PAs, a young Asian woman named Gail, volunteered for the part, was accepted, and did the shot!

No one in our group actually saw her, you understand, but just the idea of it has the men terrifically excited! Of course, they had all noticed that Gail was attractive, but just in a college-girl-in-a-baggy-sweatshirt kind of way. They had no idea that she would ever be this uninhibited. The idea that she would be willing to bare her breasts in the open air and be filmed! Suddenly they could not resist imagining it, they could not resist imagining her breasts; and surely they must have been beautiful breasts or Malick would not have chosen her. But rather than making the men more abrasive in their bad taste, this rumor has them goggle-eyed and terribly respectful in Gail's presence.

Gail's stock has gone up so high that some of the men who were formerly on a friendly, first name basis with her find they are at a loss for words in her presence. When they look at her profile, they start to wonder if she could actually be an Indian. She might be a real Indian, or she could be part Asian and part Indian. But, whatever her ethnicity, she is a definitely womanly in a way they had not formerly appreciated, and it is enough to put a lump in their throats.

After lunch, we are back at the fort for a new scene, and even after eating the equivalent of two lunches and three desserts, I am still a beaten up, hungry-looking colonist with a crutch. They haven't fired me yet, though I seem to be an incorrigible screw-up as an actor and am feeling miserable about my chances of ever qualifying for the big battle with the Indians. Why do I even want to be in the battle scene? I might end up like Randy—or worse.

The present scene is a little tricky because it involves the firing of a flint-lock pistol. Mr. Malick is in high gear. He arranges the players carefully in a triangle and works with the actor Yorick Van Wageningen so that the trajectory of his pistol is actually away from its intended target but looks on line from the angle of the camera location. (Even bullets packed as blanks sometimes injure people.) Before we begin each take, someone on the bullhorn bellows: "Fire in the hole! Fire in the hole!" which, I guess, means that a gun is about to go off so watch your head and other appendages and do not move around into the line of fire.

Out in the middle of the common area of the fort, Wingfield, played by David Thelwis, argues loudly with Smith and points a gun at him, but before he can shoot Smith, Argall, played by Yorick Van Wageningen, shoots Wingfield and drops him into the mud. The discharge of the flintlock pistol is deafening and sends up a puff of white smoke. Wingfield drops like a rock. When Wingfield/Thelwis falls, the colonists who are hanging around creep closer to see what's going on. No one wants to get in the way of these big shots with their pistols drawn, but we want to see if Wingfield is dead. No one likes Wingfield very much, so we hope this shuts him up for a while.

Thelwis does a wonderful job of seeming obnoxious, and he falls as if mortally wounded over and over again without any sign of complaint. Thelwis is very tall, and it isn't an easy matter to pick up his long, lanky frame time after time, dust himself off, and then, a few minutes later, fall down again into the mud. But he does it valiantly. I begin to feel a little sympathy for the actor, if not for the character he is playing. I am in a good spot in the middle of the yard near where I was standing this morning, and, in spite of my misery about the gum chewing, I feel that invincible red hot feeling that I may be on camera. There is a little wobble of hopefulness rising in my chest. How could I not be on camera? If they are capturing the mud around Wingfield, they are capturing the mud around me.

After several takes, there is a break and Yorick strolls over my way. He is immediately out of character and back to the jovial hale-fellow-well-met Green Bay Packers linebacker which seems his natural personality, and—never mind that he just shot Wingfield seventeen times—he gives me a pat on the back and says something to cheer me up, possibly because I resemble a decrepit old sot who can barely walk but also because, like Colin Farrell, he seems to consider me as one of his fellow actors and we are all just a happy band of brothers here, having a good time. Of course, I am flattered and grateful. Right there on the spot, I hope Yorick wins an Oscar and becomes a big star. I would follow him into battle any day—whether against Powhatan's tribe or against the Dallas Cowboys and the Washington Redskins, combined.

It is another very late night when we are finally finished and hop on the stake-bed truck for our ride back to base camp. I pack my rancid colonist's clothing in the mesh bag in Wardrobe, put on my civilian clothes without worrying about the make-up all over my face, neck, chest, and arms, and make a bee-line for my car, which is parked close in because of my very early arrival this morning.

Already other cast members are gunning their pick-ups and SUVs and whipping out and hurrying along the narrow road, headlights blazing. I am one of the few guys with just an ordinary automobile—no jacked up chassis, no giant nubby tires, no cow-catcher bumper. I unlock my car quickly, get in and back out smartly, then feel a sudden thud. The back end of my car drops several inches, and that's when I realize my back tires have gone into the ditch on the other side of the road.

I put the transmission into Drive, but there is no traction. I'm stuck. I hop out but I can't see beans. Everything is black except from the headlights and taillights of the vehicles scrambling to leave, and the taillights to one side of me rapidly disappear into the black ether, while the headlights on the other side stack up, one behind the other, shooting their lights mostly over my head into the forest. Unfortunately, my car is perpendicular to the road, and the ditches on either side are too steep and narrow for even an SUV to navigate. The exodus comes to a complete halt, and I am the culprit!

I walk around helplessly for a minute or two, and then a large Indian appears out of the darkness. He climbs down onto all fours and shines a light under my rear wheels and trunk. A couple of other Indians stand above him, watching. "Turn off the ignition!" he yells loudly. "Turn it off right now!"

I turn it off and kill my lights.

The large Indian stands up. "You backed over one of the stakes," he says. "The mutha punctured your gas tank. You're up shit crick, Man!" My emotions take a plunge. The company had erected a thin rope along this area to warn against the ditch, but in my haste I had not seen or remembered any of it in the darkness, though I had noticed it that morning. The stake had been holding up the rope, and now it was lodged in my gas tank.

"What does the rest of it look like?" I say.

"Your frame is on the road, Man. It might be bent, but I'm not sure. Your wheels are in the muck. You're not going anywhere tonight, Man. If you try to turn your bleeping gas on, it's liable to blow. So don't do it, okay?"

"Okay," I say. "But how in the hell am I going to get out of here?"

"Good question," he says. He signals to the others and the rest of them file around the front end of my car and disappear into the darkness beyond. He stays behind momentarily. "Luckily, I arrived after you did, Kemo-sabi, and parked farther down the road." He gives a little huff, not quite a chortle, and shakes his head, like *too bad you're such an idiot*, then he, too, disappears.

Now a few horns start in—from the line piling up behind me. I get down on the ground and try to size up the situation, but I can't see a thing. Two men from the pick up behind me climb out and come over to look. One of them has a flashlight. We both get down on the ground. He's a middle-aged white guy with a beard and a Virginian accent. "I heard what he said," he says. "I see the stake, but I don't think it punctured anything. I think you're all right." He's very calm and non-judgmental.

"But what if you're wrong?" I say.

"Jimmy, take the end of that bumper there. See if you can rock it any."

Jimmy rocks it a little. "See, that's touchin' it, that stake, but there's no gas on the road. I think you're all right."

"I sure hope you're right."

"Why don't you get in and start her up. We'll push her a little and try to get your tires back on the road."

"You're sure?"

"If we see any gas, we'll yell for you to cut her off. Jimmy, better lose the cigarette!" Some other men have arrived, and they take up positions behind the rear bumper, being careful not to step too far down into the ditch, which is full of water at the bottom. It's hard to tell who anybody is because everyone is in shadow.

"Okay," I say. "Here goes nothing."

I turn the key, fully expecting to be blown sky-high. Instead the engine starts up, the back-end rocks a little, then a little more, then catches the road. I hold my breath, still expecting sudden death. Nothing. I give it a little gas and square my wheels and pull right out of the ditch with the men trailing behind.

"Nice going," I say, hopping out. "Thanks a million!" I give them all high-fives. "You saved my life!" Most of them head back to their vehicles.

The man with the beard shines his light under the rear. "See, there's nuthin'. You're good to go!"

"You guys deserve a medal!" I say. "You really do."

"We'll settle for getting' home tonight," the bearded man says, though he is obviously pleased.

"Me too," I say, giving them a final grateful wave.

13

A strange thing happens when Jeannie's assistant calls to recruit my participation in the big battle scene. He says it will be five days of work in a row, and I will have to report at six in the morning every day, ready to roll. (I do the calculation: That means I will have to get up at four o'clock in the morning day after day and drive like a maniac to arrive on time.) This is the moment I have been working toward for weeks—an invitation to the big battle scene—and I did make the cut and that feels good. But the strange thing is that I hear myself saying "no" and making up some feeble excuse.

I would still like to be in the big battle scene, but I do not want to go through the torture, boredom, and humiliation of accomplishing it. I can feel it in my bones. The fact is I'm exhausted. I'm exhausted, and I know I will be even more exhausted very soon if I say yes. *Now they will probably never invite me back again for anything, and I wouldn't either, if I were in their shoes.* "This guy is a bum," I hear them saying in Richmond. "We go out of our way to toss him a morsel, and he spits in our faces." *This was my big chance, and I blew it. Now my film career is over. Oh well. Que sara sara. Life goes on, and I can sleep late next week!*

But late the next week I receive another call, and they want me back in the built fort the following Monday. The built fort! I'm not a reject, after all! I guess my unforgettable crutch work got someone's attention, and now that I'm well-rested enough to be sorely regretting that I missed the big battle scene, how can I say "no." Four o'clock in the morning! No problem!

Monday dawns and I am already on the road, half dreaming, half awake. The Interstate slides by like last week's news, already a forgotten memory before it's over. When I reach the side roads and I see the "TNW" mystery signs are still in place to mark each turn, I experience a stab of regret that this may be my last trip as a Jamestown colonist, one of the select few who knows what "TNW" means along this stretch of road.

Surely as soon as the shooting is finished, the signs and everything else will disappear, though if I were the owner of the land that was leased for the shoot, I would keep the forts and the Indian longhouse and hook up with the Jamestown Museum or Ticketron and run guided tours of the place. "See how the colonists actually lived! Stand on the very spot where Colin Farrell kissed Pocahontas!" Then after interest died down, I would just keep the built fort for my own pleasure.

I park close to base-camp and sleep-walk to the casting building and find my garb on its hanger. The shirt is stiff with dried sweat and old make-up, but I put it on anyway. Some extras and members of the cast drop off their dirty clothes to be laundered, but I am usually too tired to think about that, plus I am supposed to be dirty, right? It seems more in keeping with my character's living in his element to be wearing rank clothing, but the first few minutes of dressing in these items is a repulsive way to start the day. Also, I am so sleepy I can barely focus. If I were home I would be asleep right now and for the next two hours, and when I woke up around eight o'clock I would feel like a human being instead of a zombie.

I amble on out to the waiting stake-bed truck with the other inmates and soon we are trundling over deep ruts out to the built fort, dodging overhanging tree limbs and squinting at the sky. The morning brightness is an offense to the eyes, and once it dawns fully, the day is hot and humid but with a grey overcast. Soon we are climbing down onto the hard-packed sandy road and making our way to the fort. Once inside, we notice that carpenters are banging the finishing touches onto a platform and crow's nest arrangement in the high distant corner of the fort wall. I meander in the direction of the church and lower myself carefully onto one of the heavy ax-hewn pews.

One wall has been partially completed since the last time I was here, with a few new clapboards added, but the roof is still open to the sky and the front open to the central yard. The church offers a resting place with a full view of any activity that might be about to take place and within easy hearing distance of Mr. Malick's bullhorn. I gather from snatches of conversation I overhear from the passing PAs that the morning's work is likely to be a pan shot from the new crow's nest. I close my eyes and wait while the air and noise vibrate through my eyelids.

Shirelle appears and yells for our group to meet outside the front gate. She is in no mood to trifle. There, near the shoreline of the Chickahominy River is a small, low-roofed barn with open sides and several bales of straw stacked up. Shirelle tells us to break out the bales and to spread the straw around the barn floor and along the edges, then wait there in the barn for further instructions. Then she wheels around and marches back into the fort.

I can't quite figure out why this barn has been constructed outside the fort walls, but, because of its proximity to the waterline, it looks as if it might be a place where unloaded cargo can be stored temporarily after being unloaded from a ship or shallop. As we work laying down the itchy straw, the specter of flesh-eating bacteria in the water pops into my mind again, of course; and I am praying they are not planning another scene of colonists-in-the-dark-river-breaking-their-backs-toting-barrels-all-day. *I am not going in the water under any circumstances!*

After what seems an interminable wait, we are called back inside the fort. PAs are scurrying about, and then they place members of our motley crew at various strategic locations around the yard. I have ended up next to a barnyard enclosure near a side building that seems to be an open air kitchen. The PA gives me a shovel with a wooden blade and tells me—when the camera rolls from the platform—to pretend I am shoveling manure or working with the fence posts. One of the animal handlers lets a large pig into my pen, takes out a paint brush, and starts to paint the pig. The pig is beige-colored, and the handler is painting it black.

Today I have brought an apple. The pig-painting seems a good time to eat it, so I take the apple out of my pouch and gnaw away while leaning on the fence watching the pig being painted. When I'm finished, I ask the handler if she minds if I feed the apple core to the pig and she says, "No, go ahead." The pig takes a while to realize she is about to receive a windfall, but then she notices the apple core I am dangling in front of her and seizes it in her teeth. I am careful to avoid having my hand bitten off, and the pig and I have a happy moment. There must be some serious reason this perfectly good pig has to be black, but I have no idea what it is.

Two little boys suddenly appear in the open air kitchen area and start to play around with pots and utensils there. They are eight or nine years old and, judging from their accents, upper-class British kids. They are made up and dressed up as colonists, and they are noisy, talkative little rascals, getting into everything they can find. When they start up a game with a pitchfork, I tell them to put it back where they found it, and one of them says, "Why?"

I say, "Because I said so."

That doesn't seem quite good enough for him—I guess he's not used to taking orders from the barnyard help—so I take the pitchfork away from him and stand it up against the wall where it belonged. The boys gaze at the pitchfork longingly and then back at me out of the sides of their eyes. The taller one is on the verge of picking it up again but thinks better of it.

Malick and company are all up on the platform, surveying their domain through camera eyes, real and imaginary, and cranking the camera around into different positions on a tripod. I realize as I glance back in their direction that the angle of the roof of the kitchen building is going to obscure most of my position—something the PA did not consider when stationing me there. Since the point of my efforts is to survive and to leave something of myself on celluloid—even if at this distance it will be no larger than a flea—I take my shovel and stroll over to the middle of the range next to one of the huts, as if I know what I am doing, and park myself there to chat with one of my colleagues.

We lean on our shovels and stare back across the yard, where Jerry the suave realtor has decided to straddle the cannon and, with a silly smile on his face, is rubber-necking this way and that to see if any of the female crew members notices the size of his new equipment—the barrel of the cannon. I wonder briefly if the world is really full of forty-year-old men with the minds of high school sophomores? Everyone ignores him.

"What are you men doing here?" one of the PAs says as he walks by.

"We're trenching this hut," I say, "to keep the run-off from the roof out of the building."

"Good idea," he says, and walks on.

"All right, colonists," Mr. Malick says through his bullhorn from up on the platform. "This shot is simply going to capture a day-in-the-life at the camp, showing the colonists working away at various chores. Just ignore us and work away at your assigned tasks while the camera is rolling. We are also shooting across the distant wall of the fort to reveal some military training exercises under way at the same time. Remember: just keep busy and focus on the job at hand. We're going to do several takes. Ready?"

"That's a surprise," I say to no one in particular.

"Clear the set!" yells one of the drill sergeants. "Rolling! rolling! Action!"

I thrust my shovel into the dry earth at the base of the hut just beneath the roof line and carve out a neat trench running the length of the front of the building. The other guy is working on the side wall, but since the hut is at a diagonal from the platform, we are roughly an equal distance from the camera, more or less in the middle of the shot. I work as if my life depended on it—to avert a torrent of rainwater in my living room. Through several starts and stops, breaks and restarts, I just keep digging until I have to start filling the trench in again in order to have anything left to dig. That is when I begin to lose patience. I hate to do the same work twice. It gives me a headache.

On one of the breaks I notice the black-haired young woman from William and Mary lurking about behind the hut—still looking pissed off and miserable. I wave her over. At first she ignores me, then she comes over. "Have you had any luck?" I ask.

"No," she says, irritably.

"I was just thinking that you would make a pretty good Indian." She gives me a sharp glance as if now I have lost my mind entirely—and she was never too clear about my sanity in the first place. "I mean with your dark hair…. If you lost the glasses and with the right make-up, you could fool the camera—you could be quite convincing. It would be a way to participate—you wouldn't have to hide out the way you're doing now."

"As an Indian! No, I don't think so," she says. "Terry would never agree to that."

"How do you know if you don't ask him?" I say.

"That's not the kind of role I'm looking for anyway," she says.

"Okay," I say. She is holding out for something bigger, I guess—a starring role.

"What made you think of that, of all things?" she says, suddenly even more suspicious of my intentions.

"Just an idea," I say. "Just trying to be helpful. You don't look very happy."

She snorts. "Well, I'm not at all interested in that. Sorry."

"Okay."

"Clear the set! Clear the set!" comes the command from on high. With that, Ms. William & Mary turns and flings her bush of dark hair back over her shoulder as she retreats into the shadows in the narrow alley of space behind the row of huts.

"Any chance of getting some sunscreen over here?" I call out to one of the nearby make-up assistants. "I can feel my forehead starting to burn."

"I'll check," she says, disappearing into the darkness inside the nearby hut. In a minute, she peeks out again and whispers: "Sorry, we didn't bring any today—because of the clouds."

"Rolling. Rolling."

"Okay," I pantomime, and go back to another round of heavy trenching.

"Action!"

14

A lull overtakes us, and I notice a group of well-dressed newcomers approaching—three people in civilian clothes—who stare at us as if we are just another part of the scenery. The one who seems to be leading a tour of sorts is an attractive and chatty woman, and the couple she is talking to—a man and his wife is my guess—seem to be the persons for whom the tour was designed. These three are so different-looking than the rest of us, and so *clean*, that I can't help wondering who they are and what their intentions might be. The woman pauses near our corner and points to the camera on its tripod back on the platform, and I overhear a bit of their conversation.

The chatty woman is so full of charm and of facts and figures that I immediately size her up as one of New Line Cinema's development executives. Whoever she is, she is evidently trying to persuade the rich couple to support this or some future cinematic enterprise. Touring the set of a current production is apparently one of the perks of investing in the art form, and the wealthy couple seems to be enjoying the experience. They look us up and down as if we are a part of their prospective purchase and then cross a stretch of mud in their expensive shoes and examine the black pig in its pen.

As the trio approaches the hut next to ours, there is a yelp and shouting and several bodies suddenly running. We crane our heads to see what in the world is going on. A circle of curious PAs is forming in the area, and word filters back that a dangerous snake has been spotted—a copperhead—near where our guests were standing. The animal handler appears with a forked implement and a box and marches fearlessly to the rescue. After the snake is dispatched, there is a lot of furious talking all around and nervous laughter from our guests—oh, the excitement of it all!

I'm not feeling so well. My forehead and neck are sunburned, and my stomach feels queasy. Of course, I haven't eaten in eight hours, which could explain the light-headedness. But why the nausea and sense of malaise? More digging in the trench, more sweating through my clothes, more rolling, rolling, rolling, until, finally, the trenching and retrenching are over. The pan shot from the platform is complete in several versions, and we are free to loaf—so long as we stay out of sight.

Malick and company have something else going on in the courtyard that does not involve the colonists. I wander back and forth in the area behind the huts. Where the wall of the fort rises up, they have planted elaborate gardens that look as if they have been growing all season but were probably planted last week—exquisite cornstalks and the beautiful bulbous globes of several ripe squash. Here and there, a cucumber as well. Are they edible or are they plastic?—who knows? Will anyone ever see them? I doubt it.

I wander into one of the huts and discover it is a gathering place for several interesting women: make-up girls, PAs, Ms. William and Mary, two matronly women with English accents, who are talking animatedly, and a stunning younger woman with a cell phone in her hand. I collapse onto the lid of a cooler sitting there and squat momentarily like a fly on the wall, trying to distract myself from my queasiness by listening in. The older women seem to be directing all their conversation at the pretty younger one. It takes several seconds for my eyes to adjust to the darkness.

"Of course, little Kevin is delighted to be doing it," one of them says. "What an opportunity! We weren't really surprised he did so well in the auditions, of course. We noticed his talent years ago, and he's always done so well at school. It certainly is a trait that you have to have from birth though, wouldn't you say? It's not an ability you can ever *learn* actually, though education may improve upon it."

The younger woman nods but does not seem at all impressed by these comments. "Pardon me just a moment," she says in a lilting aristocratic voice. She flips her phone open and says: "Yes, hello. I'm calling to confirm a dinner reservation for Mr. Colin Farrell for later today.... Yes. That will be a party of ten.... Yes—some time between eight and nine o'clock. Is that too late? Fine. Thank you." She closes the phone and smiles sweetly at the woman whose conversation has been taxing her patience.

My god, I think. *It must be Colin's girlfriend!* But this woman is so sophisticated and elegant! She is clearly a higher order of human being, beautiful, charming, and intelligent and a *complete babe.* Somehow she is not quite what I expected, but then what did I expect? How would I have any clue about what to expect? Of course a man like Colin Farrell can probably attract any kind of girlfriend he wants. In my feverish state, I can feel my estimation of Colin's good taste rising exponentially.

The young woman from William and Mary, who has been leaning against the near wall, bends down towards me and says: "If the Water Manager catches you sitting on that cooler, you'll be dead, I can tell you that." There is something just a little bit self-satisfied and vindictive in her tone, which makes me regret that I ever tried to help her. But, of course, she was indeed a member of the crack Water Crew before being fired, so she probably knows all the rules a lot better than I do.

"Thanks for the warning," I say, getting up from my perch and going outside, since there is no place else to sit. *It's probably better to throw up out here anyway*, I'm thinking.

Ms. William and Mary follows me out. "Who was that woman in there?" I ask her, "the one on the phone?

"Oh, that's Colin's sister," she says knowingly.

"I thought it might be his girlfriend," I say stupidly. My head feels very hot. She winces at me and turns to leave.

"No, it's his sister," she says, turning back momentarily, "and she's his manager too, I've heard."

"Wow," I say, trying to take in this new information. *Two geniuses in the same family…and both of them exceptionally good-looking. How often does that happen?*

"You don't look so good," she says.

"I'm not feeling too well," I say. I stagger a few steps into the garden patch, grabbing at a loose corn stalk, and upchuck all over my shoes and one of the lovely orange squashes. "Yuck," I say, too loudly, then vomit a little bit more. I shake my head back and forth like a horse in agony and spit several times, trying to get it all out. *Now if I can just find something I can use to wipe off my shoes*, I'm thinking. *I wonder if I finally ruined them?* When I turn around, I find I am alone. Ms. William and Mary has disappeared.

I duck through a slot in the fort wall and walk slowly out into the fennel field. The fennel is higher than my head and seems to go on forever. Several mystery paths have been trodden down, heading off god knows where. I certainly don't feel like exploring very far, but I am just so bored and tired and sick I have to keep moving. I could be home right now, lying on my own couch, instead of wandering through a field of impressive weeds when I should probably be lying down with a thermometer in my mouth. Suddenly I miss my wife with an intensity that feels like a physical pain. Oh, to be home! I could go home right now! I *should* probably go home right now. The idea of it is like a shot of adrenaline.

    I circle around the fort and head out to the front gate area in hopes of finding Shirelle. Sure enough, she is standing between the low barn full of straw and the shore line, staring at a shallop that has just floated in along the bank. A couple of guys are hurling the end of a rope in her direction. Just what I feared! This afternoon they are going to herd us into the drink!

    I accelerate towards Shirelle just as she turns around and heads back towards the fort. I see the front gate is open and whatever filming was going on is at a standstill. I give her a little wave and approach her with as miserable an expression on my face as I can conjure up, hoping she will take sympathy upon me and give me permission to leave. There is nothing else in her line of sight that is moving except me.

    I am less than an arms length from Shirelle when I open my mouth to explain myself, but Shirelle keeps on walking as if she doesn't even see me. Apparently, I am invisible! I stop dead in my tracks and turn around and call after her. But she ignores that too. All I see is her backside departing rapidly towards the fort and the blue bandana in her hair flapping in the breeze. Must be some important mission she is on, some serious deadline she is worrying about, or something she is pissed off about—and she is pissed off about almost everything most of the time. Or maybe she could tell from my expression what I was about to say, and she didn't want to deal with it.

    But I do not like being ignored. Who does? It makes me furious. That's it! I've had it! I turn in the direction of the road back to base camp and start marching! If I have to walk two or three miles back to base camp with a 104 degree fever in this stifling heat and with a bad sunburn to boot, throwing up along the way, I will—because I am going home right now and no one is going to stop me! I tried to tell Shirelle about my condition, but Shirelle did not want to hear it. So I am doing this on my own initiative, and my film career is probably over. Who cares! Will anybody even notice I am gone? Probably not, and think of the money they will save!

"He walked off the set!" someone says in an imaginary conversation inside my head.

"Oh my God! What are they going to do to him now?"

"Well, it's not as if he's Colin bleeping Farrell after all! He can be replaced. He was just an extra. But I'll tell you one thing: He won't be taking lunch in *this* town again. You can count on that!"

Suddenly a white van pulls up beside me and stops. The passenger door flies open, and the gristly old guy from the prop truck nods hello. "You want a ride back to camp?" he says. "Climb in." His demeanor is so friendly compared to our earlier meetings that I hardly recognize him.

"I don't mind walking," I say. "I'm sick."

"Better climb in then," he says. "Come on."

"What are you doing out here?" I say, climbing in.

"Not a thing," he says. "Just heading back to camp. Saw you and thought you might need a ride."

"Well, I appreciate it," I say. He starts up the van and we roll along towards camp. "I just threw up in a squash patch and walked off the set. I'm not feeling too hot."

He nods. He already knows. Someone sent him after me.

"The heat is deceptive out there today," he says philosophically. "Not to mention the humidity. I think we'll probably get some rain tonight."

"I wouldn't doubt it," I say.

When we get back to camp, it's mostly deserted. I thank my benefactor in the van and climb the steps of the casting building and go straight to ardrobe. I take off my shoes and wipe them down with paper towels. I strip off my colonist's clothes and pack them in their mesh bag and get dressed as fast as I can manage. I want to be gone before they break for lunch. Then I write a note for Shirelle and attach it to the day's pay slip: "Dear Shirelle, I got sick and had to go home. Sorry for leaving in the middle of things. I enjoyed working with you. I left at 2 P.M. Best wishes, Joe Bellamy."

15

Epilogue

The last call I receive from Jeannie is not long after I vomit on my shoes and storm off the set. Jeannie acts as if she doesn't know or care a thing about that. Maybe she doesn't. She says they definitely need my services the very next day as a stand-in for Christopher Plummer! The set is in Richmond, where they are shooting some scenes of London, and I will need to report, as usual, at 6 A.M.

Richmond is even farther away from my home than the previous base camp, so it does not take me long to thank her and say no. I mean, a stand-in makes $10/hour and eats with the crew, but a stand-in is not at all likely to actually be *in the film*. For me, it is not about the money. It is all about art, immortality, and sleeping late.

I say I just can't get up that early anymore. The Richmond location would mean waking up at 3:30 in the morning, I tell her. Jeannie says everyone else has to do it too. "Not the people in

Richmond," where *she* lives, I might have said. But I didn't. Or I could have said: "Surely you can find someone else who is exactly 6' tall and weighs 170 pounds." But I didn't say that either. I just say, "I know it, but I can't. Thanks anyway, Jeannie." And that is that—the end of my movie career. When my last check arrives in the mail, I see that they paid me for the whole day that last day when I left early. Was that a goodbye present from Shirelle, a kind of belated apology, or just an accounting error? I don't know.

The World Premiere of *The New World*, starring Colin Farrell, Christopher Plummer, Christian Bale, and a new young actress named Qorinka Kilcher, is held in Williamsburg, Virginia, on December 24, 2005—several weeks before the nationwide release date, which is set to be early in 2006. My wife and I are desperate to see the completed film, but I am not one of the locals invited. After all, I was only an extra—plus I chewed gum when I shouldn't have, and I wasn't willing to fight the Indians when it really mattered or stand in for Mr. Plummer at the end if it meant getting up at an ungodly hour. What do I expect?

So it is that I show up with my wife on the opening night of the nationwide release of *The New World* in Virginia Beach along with everyone else in America who wanted to see it on January 20th, 2006. Quite a few movie-goers are interested apparently. The theater is packed, and we are lucky to find seats.

During the year, we have read rumors about Malick's trials and tribulations. First, we read, that the film would be released by November or December to put it in contention for an Oscar nomination but then, without explanation, it was delayed. Our hopes were way up and then were dashed.

Later we read that the finished film was three-and-a-half hours long—perhaps four—and Malick loved it but the studio didn't. Later we read that the studio was forcing Malick to reduce the film to two-and-a-half hours. Later, we read there were rumors the studio had taken the film away from Malick and were cutting it themselves, changing it from a great classic film into an ordinary piece of Hollywood drivel. Personally, I was rooting for Malick.

Possibly, the longer classic version would be released later as a "Director's Cut" on DVD. I certainly hoped so because I assumed I would end up either on the cutting room floor, or, if I was extremely lucky, in one of the deleted scenes. The shorter the film, the less likely I was to be in it!

Another problem that we read about was that the scenes between Colin Farrell and Qorinka Kilcher were too hot and had to be re-shot in order for the film to receive an R rating. Whether they returned to the fennel fields of Virginia to do this was not disclosed, but I could not imagine how they would have been able to accomplish it otherwise. Qorinka was, after all, only fourteen or fifteen at the time of the filming, and so, though she seemed quite womanly, she was underage. The last thing they needed was some prudish reviewer or film board member complaining about child abuse.

Back at the theatre where we are awaiting the showing, the woman sitting next to my wife turns to her and says, "My husband was an extra in this film! That's why we're here tonight. We want to see if he's in the final cut."

"Good luck," my wife says. She looks at me and smiles. I glance over toward the woman's husband, but I don't recognize him from Adam. He must have been in some other part of the movie.

The lights go down, and the screen lights up.... Now we have the Virginia Beach premier of *The New World* in living color, and what a feast for the eyes it is! But it is hard to watch. I want to enjoy it, but I can't help being distracted by wondering when and if I will see myself or any of my buddies. It is not easy to watch the film and to also watch for the appearance of one obscure actor who may or may not be chewing gum at the moment of his greatest triumph. The film flies along, and there is no stopping it!

Also, on this particular night, the theater must be full of *New World* extras because every so often—for no apparent reason—applause and cheering break out in some corner of the room when the friend, husband, lover, brother, sister, father, or little cabin boy extra suddenly appears on the screen. For this reason alone, the audience is in high spirits. After all, most of us had been waiting for over a year to witness the outcome of our labors, and now the grand occasion is upon us. I can't imagine what any ordinary film-goers might be thinking about the sudden outbursts and the festive mood. They must think they are in the midst of an enormous wedding party or a field trip by the local mental hospital.

I discover that most of my contribution, such as it is, is in the first half-hour of the film. My best efforts may be on the cutting room floor (and now in the trash), but, hey, I did make it to the big-time—if only for a few seconds!

(1) About one full second of me as a strong-armed colonist lifting up a large log to build the wall of the fort, (2) About half a second hoeing in the garden patch—mostly just my hands on the hoe actually, (3) More than one second: Walking with the "Jamestown elders" when Newport (Christopher Plummer) explains that he's going back to London for a while and leaving Smith in charge of military operations. This was my very first scene when, you may recall, I wasn't filling in the tableau properly until the blonde drill sergeant yelled at me several times. The camera is mostly on Newport and Smith, but I am there in a hat with a feather in it for quite some time. At one point my back fills the entire screen. You'd have to be more familiar with my back than I am to recognize me, but my wife did. (4) When Argall shoots Wingfield, I am hobbling on a crutch in the background after the smoke clears. I am one of the starving colonists. No hat. No feather. No gum. (This was after I threw out the gum.) I look about a hundred years old and crippled, but this is my most obvious appearance—a very clear shot throughout most of the scene. That's it—a very strange form of immortality that I would not have wished for but can hardly complain about.

Rumor is that the DVD version will be an hour longer, so my wife is waiting eagerly to catch a longer glimpse of me then—though she may do that any day of the week at no charge.

I like the film. I think it is both lyrical and, in some instances, shockingly realistic, probably the most accurate portrayal of what it must have been like at that exact time and place that has ever been filmed. Malick has a great eye for beauty and for strangeness. He might need a little help with narrative, but, c'mon, the man is a genius. I don't quite understand why the box office has been relatively poor. I don't think the film deserves that. We see so few ambitious and original films these days, you'd think there would be some celebrating for this one. There was a time when this film would have been considered among the best of the year—without question. I'll tell you one thing: It's on my list of the Ten Best without any qualifications—maybe even Ten Best of All Time.

When the showing is over, I squint intensely at dispersing members of the crowd, hoping to spot Randy or his brother or Michener or Timothy or any one of my former colleagues—to give them a high-five. But I do not recognize a single soul. They are probably in other theaters, somewhere else in southeastern Virginia, where similar scenes are undoubtedly occurring. This film had a lot of extras, hundreds of them, mostly anonymous folks like me whose names were not even listed in the credits but who worked hard for minimum wage, got up too early in the morning, and put up with a lot of horse shit in hopes of participating in a work of art, a work of lasting beauty and significance. Would I do it again? Probably not, but there are a lot worse ways to spend your summer vacation.

Several months later, I read in the newspaper that the next big movie in Virginia is going to be an eight-part HBO production of *John Adams*, and Tom Hanks is involved. This is huge! I stop reading the paper to let the full import of it sink in. Tom Hanks is a guy I wouldn't mind getting to know.

It is not known if Hanks himself will play John Adams[1] or when production will begin, but they will most likely be filming in Williamsburg! the newspaper says. Williamsburg is not that far away! I could probably sleep until 5 A.M.

John Adams is actually a distant relative of mine! I could definitely see myself as a member of the Continental Congress! or dressed up as an Indian dumping tea into Boston Harbor! or taking a bullet at the Old North Bridge, winging a Redcoat as I slide over the railing, then collapsing into the stream and dying a slow, agonizing death.

Ordinarily, I wouldn't give it a moment's thought, but this is one film I might consider doing. *I'm experienced.* They definitely might need an extra like me!

---

[1] Paul Giamatti was eventually cast as John Adams, and Laura Linney was cast as Abigail Adams.

www.ingramcontent.com/pod-product-compliance
Lightning Source LLC
Chambersburg PA
CBHW031654040426
42453CB00006B/300